Dear
well do
really fa
with this

from
Anna x

The Dirtbags

First published in 2023

Jay Jackson is the pen name of
Author Anna Friend

First Edition

ISBN 978-1-8383722-5-5

Quirky Bird Books

For Jack & Billy, my amazing kids

And all the fantastic Dirtbags

I've known

x

Characters

Taylor	he/him
Quinn	they/them
Joy	she/her
Old Joe	he/him
Captain America the Cat	he/him

One

The Dirtbags were cool. Really cool. Amazingly COOL. The Dirtbags were so cool that if they met cool say, in a park or on a street, cool would stop, wide-eyed, open mouthed and whisper in a voice filled with awe and wonder, "YOU'RE SOOOO COOL," and The Dirtbags would simply reply, "We know," and keep walking. In a REALLY COOL WAY.

OK. THAT'S A LIE.

They weren't very cool.

They weren't cool at all actually.

I mean they were almost cool because they were so uncool. But still, that meant that they were not cool.

Yeah. The Dirtbags were the most cool uncool kids in the school.

The Dirtbags were the kind of kids that made the other kids move aside to let them walk through and not because they were cool but because they were SUPER NOT COOL.

The Dirtbags were the kids who, when you got paired with them

to Do Science or

brainstorm a topic in English or

as a teammate in PE (the absolute worst)

you'd roll your eyes and you might even say, "But Miss, urgh, I hate working with them."

Which would be exceptionally rude and not OK and the class teacher would tell you off and make you do it anyway and everyone else in the class would be relieved because they didn't have to work with a Dirtbag.

These were the Dirtbags. Every school has them.

The Dirtbags are the ones that grow up to own huge IT corporations, or invent amazing world changing gadgets.

The Dirtbags are the ones that grow up to be creative geniuses and stand in front of huge crowds and give TED talks but at school the Dirtbags are just the Dirtbags.

Not cool. Not exciting. Not someone to be friends with. Not someone to stand in the lunch queue with. Not someone to do your Science homework with.

Just. Not. Someone.

These Dirtbags met on a Saturday, which was kind of surprising considering they'd been at school together for ALMOST THREE YEARS. Some in the same classes.

However it was one Saturday that they met, at Old Joe's Comic Store, in town. The name says it all really. The shop itself had been there for years. No one really remembered it opening, certainly none of the parents of the Dirtbags had any recollection of Old Joe's Comic Store ever arriving in Feckleston-on-the Wold. However, here it was, an outcast of a shop, which, some might say, is why it suited the Dirtbags.

So every Saturday the Dirtbags would visit the comic store, browsing through pages of Marvel adventures, furtively eyeing each other amongst the adventures of Batman and Spiderman, vintage Beanos and Dennis the Menace.

On this Saturday the Dirtbags were the only three people in the shop. This was not unusual. No one else ever really went into Old Joe's Comic Store. Everyone else was online, checking things out, liking and subscribing. Being COOL.

But these three were here.

One of them was deeply engrossed in episode two of *The New Adventures of Spiderman.*

Sitting almost directly opposite them was a girl. She had episode one of the same series and every now and again she would let out a wild laugh, like a caged animal had found a way to tickle itself. Sometimes they caught each other's eye and she laughed then too. He attempted to smile but instead pulled a face like he was trying to hold a fart in and then they both looked away.

Unbeknownst to them, there was in fact another in the shop. This person was sitting on the floor beneath the large racks of comics, and they had found what can only be described as a one-of-a-kind.

It was the first and only edition of the brand-new *Adventures of the Amazing GLITTERMAN.* The reason it was the only edition was because shortly after it was made, the writers realised the following:

The main hero in this comic was made of glitter and this was a fundamental flaw against there ever being an ongoing series of the amazing Glitterman.

You can't have a superhero made of glitter because if they come across anything – wind, fire, water, any of these things will destroy them, straightaway.

And you can't really argue with that, you know. I mean, it's Science.

And this person, sitting on the floor, knew it. Even though they hadn't learnt a lot in Science. They learnt that.

Anyhow, under the rack they sat, delicately turning the pages of the ancient comic, terrified that any moment it would disintegrate entirely, leaving the world forever ignorant to the adventures of amazing GLITTERMAN.

Suddenly, just above their head, a fierce argument erupted. Sticking their head out, they saw that the boy and the girl were standing right by the rack under which they were cowering.

"Absolutely NO WAY," said the boy, still trying to maintain his composure.

"Yes WAY!"

"NO. There's no way that in episode one, Peter Parker and Electro are friends. ABSOLUTELY NO WAY."

"Well, here it is. On page five. That is clearly Electro, standing with Peter in the Science lab, before he even has his powers."

"But that has never been part of his origin story and Electro doesn't even feature in episode two."

"Who's that then?" the girl said, pointing at the comic open in the boy's hand.

"Wha... what?" The boy erupted into what can only be described into the most fake and awkward laugh ever, whilst eyeing the page with a sense of panic. "That's not Electro, that's... that's..."

A huge, deep laugh interrupted their discussion and filled the air in an eerie and ominous way. The boy and the girl froze. They both stood very still and, beneath the rack, breath was held.

"Of course Electro and Peter Parker are friends!" said Old Joe, quietly, shuffling towards the pair.

"Isn't that how all enemies are made? Your greatest friend becomes your worst enemy?" He eyed them both and tapped the shoe of the one that lurked beneath.

"Or sometimes it's the other way round." He pulled out episode three. "Look here's The Lizard, helping Peter in the library."

The boy and the girl stopped, laughed, then grabbed the comic from Old Joe's hand. As if some unspoken truce was made they both slid to the floor and started reading together. But as they turned the first page, they became acutely aware they were not alone. They turned and found that staring back at them was a surprisingly orange face. Silence. And then.

"Want a Cheeto?" said a voice that belonged to the person beneath the giant comic rack.

"Thanks," said the boy and girl together, then reached for the bag.

The sound of munching broke the awkward silence.

"I'm Quinn by the way," said the orange face.

"Taylor," the boy said, licking his fingers

The girl took another Cheeto then grinned.

“I’m Joy,” she said

These were the Dirtbags.

Two

Taylor is the kind of kid that gets called nice. A lot. Always by teachers and parents, adults of any sort really.

Taylor hates the word nice.

"Nice?" he said to his best friends, Quinn and Joy as they waited in the queue at The Snack Shack in town, "Nice? I'm not nice, I'm mean and cool and stuff."

Taylor lived with his family in a totally ordinary street, in a pretty ordinary house. He shared this house with his Mum, Dad Jason and younger brother Ollie, who lived exclusively in his pants.

Taylor also shared his house with his cat Mr Crabbs. True, this is not a great name for a cat, but if you saw him walk, you'd understand. Plus Mr Crabbs' best friend, which was an almond.

So this was what Taylor was dealing with on a daily basis. Ollie in his pants, Mr Crabbs and his almond.

Oh, and school.

Taylor actually didn't hate school. I mean, if you took all the other kids out of it and just left his fave teachers plus best friends Quinn and Joy then school would be AMAZING!

His absolute favourite person in school was Mr Fineline, his art teacher.

When Mr Fineline described Taylor's work, something gurgled and bubbled in Taylor's tummy. It reminded him of that time when his mum went all experimental in the kitchen, but this time it didn't end in the bathroom; it was more like he'd won a prize or was sitting on top of some great mountain.

On a school day, Taylor spent much of his time constructing and planning his creations in his head. His teachers often said he was a daydreamer, but in reality, he wasn't dreaming. He was building and landscaping. He was the architect of huge imaginary worlds which he brought to life in incredible detail. His bedroom was littered with sketches of every inch of a detailed and incredible world, pinned across his noticeboard. Surfaces were transformed into wild alien jungles, huge industrial landscapes, worlds coloured like rainbows, and they were extraordinary.

Quinn and Joy would marvel over his creations and the three of them would make up adventures and games based on the worlds that Taylor created. They would sit in their hideout, sharing all the weird and unusual snacks that can be found at The Snack Shack and talk for hours, tracking through imaginary pathways, battling monsters and making world saving discoveries. The three of them created the best stories.

Taylor would describe the world, in intricate detail, from giant fungi to tiny, winged creatures. Joy had a knack for people and would introduce wild and crazy characters.

But the best.

The absolute best storyteller of all of them.

Was Quinn.

Quinn loved their friends. They made them feel safe and they didn't have a lot of that elsewhere in their life. Other things that Quinn loved were comic books and science. They also loved Cheetos coz they were super cheesy and made their face go slightly orangey.

So, all these things. Yes.

Things that Quinn didn't like included PE (urgh), being outside (double urgh), wetness of any kind (giant URGH), so you get the picture.

However, the GREATEST THING ON EARTH, in Quinn's opinion was Dungeons and Dragons which they had discovered at Old Joe's, one Saturday, before Taylor and Joy were a thing and definitely before they became their best ever friends in the whole world.

Dungeons and Dragons was a table-top role play game, where you rolled a dice to discover what was going to happen to your character and the Dungeon Master (coolest person ever!) would tell you all about your journey and the witches and warlocks you'd meet. Sitting there in Old Joe's dusty back room, Quinn had lined up the miniature figures, admiring the beautiful detail. They thumbed through the character sheets and felt a rush of excitement reading about banshees and mages, and then, the best thing of all, the dice.

The dice used in Dungeons and Dragons were EXTREMELY SUPER COOL.

Purple ones, green ones, yellow ones, six-sided, twelve-sided and the absolute top dice – the twenty-SIDED!

"Why don't you take it all home?" said Old Joe to Quinn. "It's not doing nothing sat there."

Quinn immediately said yes, thank you very much, and packed it all into their backpack. They had a cousin who they knew would love it but they only saw them once a year at the annual family get together, a totally boring event which took place in a small corner of England where no fun could possibly exist.

One year, their cousin, Max, made it all better by suggesting they go on a walk but actually what they did was sneak into an old church and made up characters and talked about STUFF. Max's STUFF was very different from Quinn's STUFF but the fact that they both had STUFF made the whooshy, wibbly feeling in Quinn's head go away.

This also made this the best family get together ever for Quinn, and found themselves dancing to the music inside their head.

Just like Joy.

Joy was often described as' a bit much' by other people, particularly her preschool teacher, after Joy had interpreted the instruction "paint whatever you like" literally and proceeded to paint the table, her chair, parts of the floor around her and Charlie, her best friend at the time.

For the first years at least, Joy thought her name was AND JOY.

Like one word.

ANDJOY.

This was because Jane, being the older child, was always introduced first and then, like a kind of afterthought it was "and Joy".

She was only corrected when, on her first day of preschool, her teacher was taking the register and Joy sat, fidgeting, waiting for her name to be called. Eventually Mrs Lilliput said gently, "Joy? This is where you say 'Yes, miss'."

And Joy realised she was called Joy, just Joy, which to be honest she liked much better.

Joy found sitting still VERY DIFFICULT.

When they were babies, this was a funny and cute aspect of Joy's personality but as she grew older it tested her parents' patience a little too much, and now that she was at school, it made things even trickier.

That and the fact that she was clumsy. Well, just kind of offbeat really, sort of out of step with the rest of the world.

IN HER HEAD Joy could see how everything was connected to the beat, and IN HER HEAD, she was mastering it all. She would go home and practise, but when it came to being in a line with eleven other dancers and moving with everyone, at the same time, with the same moves, again and again and again, it… made her head hurt. And her body didn't feel like water or lightning, so she stopped.

UNTIL.

Cheerleading Squad Tryouts.

Joy had secretly attended cheerleading training in the gym every Thursday. Joy would sneak into the gym, squish herself into the space between the bin and the seating, and watch every move. This sometimes meant she was overwhelmed with the smell of hotdogs (Week A) or vegan curry (Week B) but it was all worth it.

Joy was absolutely fascinated by the flips and the throws that formed part of the cheerleading routines.

Joy regularly flew through the air as part of the Dirtbags' parkour training which was actually just around Old Joes, from sofa to table and across the counter.

It's fair to say that Joy TOTALLY ANNIHILATED THE COURSE.

Joy became a blur of arms and legs, transformed into some sort of flying ninjutsu master, creating shapes with her body, never before seen in Feckleston-on-the Wold. Taylor and Quinn's jaws dropped as she twisted mid-air, backflipped onto the counter and leapt THROUGH THE AIR. S

So this was when Joy decided to go to the tryouts, encouraged by Taylor and Quinn.

This was also when they invented the Emergency Bucket as they all hugged really hard and Quinn said they "needed to go".

So they all let go. Really quickly. And found a bucket.

THE EMERGENCY BUCKET

This arrangement had become a necessity when they realised that the combination of hanging out all day, plus no bathroom resulted in either:

a) someone having to leave early and go home, just to use the toilet

b) going to the chip shop next door and asking to use their toilet, thus breaking their cover.

So the following rules were created;

1. Only for emergency use, when you absolutely could not hold it in

2. ABSOLUTELY NO NUMBER TWOS – this rule was non-negotiable!

3. This arrangement should never be spoken of.

Three

Old Joe was born Joseph Dabrowski. He arrived with a suitcase in 1964 and worked hard to live a good life. Joe would turn his hand to anything: carpentry, shop work, farming, brickwork, gardening – anything at all, but his day really began when he returned home, made a simple dinner for one and took out his prized collection of rare and vintage comics.

When he had inherited a small sum of money he took his chance and Old Joe's Comic Shop was born, on the high street of Feckleston-on-the-Wold, and his passion for superheroes found its home.

At first the shop was bustling with customers, some coming from far away to enquire about first editions, marvel at the

Marvel collections, and slowly Joe's little shop gained a reputation for being a quirky destination for all comic enthusiasts.

And Joe hadn't been old. He was just Joe, happy to be amongst people each day, living a life that he had only dreamt of. He moved into the flat above the shop, bought a cat and life took on a slow and gentle rhythm. Captain America, his cat, would wake him each morning and Joe would reach for his glasses and make them both breakfast. Then he would open the shop.

At first, especially on Saturdays Joe would arrive downstairs to find a queue of eager customers waiting and chatting outside the door. When they saw him they would cheer as he waved and jangled his keys.

But over the years, the queues became smaller and smaller, and as the internet grew, business dwindled and Joe no longer arrived in his shop to cheers and excitement. The store became older and uncared for, and so did Joe.

Therefore it was a surprise that one Wednesday, Joe found himself at the centre of an altercation. After popping upstairs to fetch a ham sandwich, he returned to the shop to find a school kid standing there, holding Captain America and looking like they might cry, or burst into song. Old Joe couldn't decide and wasn't interested in either.

"That's my cat," Old Joe said, as a statement.

"Right, yes," said the kid, still standing very still, "she, uh, they just kind of climbed up, here."

"I'm allergic to cats," said the child and then sneezed, causing Captain America to leap furiously away and then peer back, with an offended look on his face.

Both Old Joe and the kid stood, looking at the other for a little while. Old Joe noticed that the kid's face was a little bit sweaty AND a little bit orange.

Suddenly the door of the shop swung open and a group of kids burst in and, as quick as a flash, orange face dashed under one of the giant racks.

"You seen a kid come in here?" said the largest kid.

Old Joe noted the tie, the blazer, the school logo, all the same as the ones worn by the child who was now hidden just a few feet away. The boy who spoke had a look in his eye that Old Joe recognised and didn't like.

He moved forward and stood directly in front of the large rack, obscuring any view they might have of the small figure whose breath was now held.

"Get out," Old Joe said quietly, "get out of my shop."

No one moved.

The air in the room seemed to shudder.

Old Joe stood still, eyes on the bully that loomed in front of him and the kid on the floor felt their heart pounding.

The room seemed to get darker, the wind whipped against the windows.

Everyone stopped.

And then, after what seemed like an eternity, the kids lost interest and dawdled away till it was just the largest one left. Old Joe stepped forward, hoping the boy would retreat, the kid beneath the rack bit their lip and waited and then suddenly the bully turned on his heels and left, slamming the door behind him.

Everything was silent and eventually the kid crawled out from the space beside Old Joe's feet.

The two strangers stood and looked at each other. An unspoken moment passed between them. Finally Old Joe spoke. "They looking for you then?" he said, resisting the urge to dust this kid down.

"No, I mean, I don't know. Maybe," said the kid, embarrassed by the attention. To create a diversion they thrust their hand out and said "I just came in here, to buy - this!", grabbing the nearest comic.

Old Joe smiled and gently removed the cellophane package from their hand.

"This, my dear, must be treated with care. This is episode forty-seven of *The New Adventures of Spiderman* where not only does he come face to face with Green Goblin, but also on page sixteen, the artist made a mistake which means it's very rare." Joe gestured to the price tag and Quinn gasped.

"Do you like comics?" Old Joe said then paused. "What is your name?"

"Quinn," the kid said, then, "Yeah, I love them, me and my dad, well, we used to read stuff together all the time, you know, when I was younger."

"And now you are too old for comics?" Old Joe asked, raising an eyebrow at Quinn.

"Uh, no, it's just…" Quinn trailed off, suddenly lost in thought. "Actually, do you have anything that costs a little bit less?"

Old Joe considered the kid for a moment, then said, "What do you like?"

And so began a conversation that found this unusual pair talking and laughing and searching through the racks of comic books until they found the perfect one for Quinn's dad's birthday.

It also was the beginning of an arrangement that saw Quinn visit Old Joe's each day after school to clean and rearrange the racks and make tea (they'd never done this before), go shopping for milk or ham, feed Captain America (at a distance) all to pay for the vintage Batman comic that Quinn so proudly wrapped and presented to their dad for his birthday.

And now Quinn was in their favourite place in the store, underneath rack five, eating Cheetos and smiling to themselves when the door swung open and in walked two blazers.

Four

Just to be clear, Taylor and Joy hadn't walked in TOGETHER.

They arrived at Old Joe's Comic Store at the same time but that did not mean they arrived TOGETHER.

Of course, Joy knew who Taylor was. They'd been in the same bottom English group all year, Taylor because, although he loved reading, he didn't really like talking or writing about it, and Joy because she found words tricky.

And Quinn knew who they both were. She was the one who never got picked in PE and became 'ball monitor', whatever that was, and he had been the face for the primary school's 'LET'S LEARN' campaign two years ago and had never been allowed to forget it. Taylor's face had been made into a thousand memes which had flown around the school like wildfire and Quinn had seen them all. Quinn thought about saying hi but by this stage, the two were both sitting, studying some random Spiderman editions and Quinn remembered the stories of Glitterman that Old Joe had told them about and that was now sat in their lap, waiting to be seen.

Quinn carefully licked their fingers clean and turned to page one.

What followed was as documented previously, an event which would bring these three together in a mutual love of all things comic and snack related as well as people to fit 'not fitting in' with.

So this is where it all began. From that one meeting and the next few months where Taylor, Quinn and Joy became a regular feature at Old Joe's and, despite all his grumblings and moaning about the fact they never ever bought anything, Joe loved them being there and looked forward to 3.30 each day when the bell would ping as they entered the shop and they would walk in with all their life and chatter and noise. Old Joe would listen to them as they talked about school and people, their lessons that day, how much they hated PE or French and then eventually the four of them would settle into a comfortable silence as they sat, either all together, huddled round the counter, or like satellites, scattered round the room, chuckling and gasping as they devoured the stories of bravery, disaster and triumph. All of this until five o'clock and then Old Joe would jangle his keys and say, with a smile, "Get out of here, you Dirtbags," and off they went, till the next day.

On Saturdays the Dirtbags would set themselves challenges, like, who could read the most or the fastest or sometimes they would act out their favourite stories.

They not only read episode one, two and three of *The New Adventures of Spiderman* but systematically rearranged the comics into super awesome categories like:

- MOST AWESOME INTRODUCTION OF A NEW CHARACTER
- MOST SURPRISING ENDING
- MOST EPIC USE OF HOUSEHOLD ITEMS AS WEAPONS

And their absolute favourite:

- THE DIRTBAGS RECOMMEND…

A selection of their favourite comics which they regularly argued over but which included, at the agreement of all three of them *THE AMAZING ADVENTURES OF GLITTERMAN, THE HERO OF OUR TIME.*

By this time, Old Joe was happy to let them do what they wanted in the shop and over the years he spent more and more time upstairs and less in the shop.

This meant that the Dirtbags also learnt to:

- Empty Captain America's litter tray (worst job EVER)
- Make ham sandwiches with LOADS of butter (best job EVER)
- Use the till, on the extremely unusual occasion that a customer came in
- Use a hoover (weird), a washing machine (boring) and the toilet brush (urgh)

Taylor also spent an entire half term customising the counter hoping that this would make Old Joe want to spend a little more time with them all.

Even though he said very little, the Dirtbags missed Old Joe. They missed the way he would moan at them for cluttering up his shop and not giving him any peace but when they went to grab their bags he would find a reason for them to stay, just a little bit longer. They missed the way he would always say the right thing, when they arrived and were cross about some great injustice that ruined their life.

"What other people think of you is none of your business" he would say, "just live your life for you and no-one else."

Or:

"Every single thing that you do, will lead you to the life you want. Regret nothing, trust your instincts."

This he said to all of them in a rare moment, when he spent most of the day in the shop. He ate his sandwich and made tea and they all took turns to make him laugh.

Quinn made Old Joe laugh the most and these two could often be found, in the back room, creased up together over one of their favourite comics, tears streaming from Old Joe's eyes.

Quinn and Joe, thick as thieves.

Taylor sometimes felt a bit left out by this incredible intergenerational friendship although in his heart he knew how much Quinn needed it and he loved Quinn, which made the whole thing OK.

It might have been another reason why, having spent so much time drawing and painting the counter, Taylor felt really disappointed when Joe came down to shut the shop and didn't even notice. He didn't see that all the colours matched the colours of the shop and that Taylor had carefully crafted the landscape to include all of Joe's favourite things with Captain America (the cat) at the centre, with Old Joe by his side. Old Joe didn't see any of this but just shuffled painfully across the floor, barely looking up and the three of them picked up their stuff and wandered over to the door, waiting for their cue not to leave. But it never came, Old Joe said nothing.

As they were leaving, without warning and without really knowing why, Quinn stopped and hugged Old Joe.

The pair stopped and looked at each other for a moment, Taylor and Joy standing close by and then eventually Joe smiled a tiny smile.

"Bye," he said and shut the door and the three of them were left, standing outside their favourite place in the world, feeling like something had happened but not knowing what that was.

For the next week, the Dirtbags stood outside Old Joe's waiting to hear the jangle of keys and to be greeted by an impatient Captain America, but the door never opened and eventually Taylor, Quinn and Joy stopped waiting.

Three weeks later, as they made their way home Quinn stopped and pointed to a notice, pinned to the door. The three of them approached and stopped short. After a moment Taylor read the notice out loud:

"Funeral Notice

Thursday 17th May

Chapel Haven Funeral Home

4pm

Funeral of Joseph 'Old Joe' Dabrowski

All Welcome"

Taylor, Quinn and Joy stood still for what felt like the longest time. Without saying anything Quinn reached for both their hands and Joy rested her head on Quinn's shoulder. Quinn's shoulders shook and silent tears rolled down their face. It started to rain but the Dirtbags just stood, their heads bowed, sad for a friend that was now lost to them.

"We should go," said Taylor, "we should go to the funeral."

And they all agreed, despite not really having any idea what to do or how to get there.

And that's when they heard him. Captain America.

It was unmistakable. The yowling and scratching of the door, like he knew they were just on the other side.

"What should we do?" said Joy. "He probably hasn't been fed for days, maybe weeks."

Taylor shrugged his shoulders. "What can we do?" He tried the door. "It's all locked up."

But Quinn was off, heading towards the alley that took you round the back of the high street, and Taylor and Joy quickly followed.

When they joined Quinn they were scrabbling around amongst the plants and hanging baskets which once made up what Joe referred to as his 'English garden', but were now overgrown with weeds and litter from the neighbourhood. Finally Quinn pulled out a key, with a huge Hulk keyring attached. and placed it into the backdoor.

Before they had even reached the shop Captain America was upon them, weaving in and out of their feet and purring like an engine but the three of them were unable to get into Old Joe's flat to find cat food as the door had been locked with another sign posted: PROBATE PENDING.

"What does that mean?" said Joy

Quinn and Taylor shrugged and Quinn bent down to stroke the cat, who continued to mew.

"We gotta feed him," said Joy, "Has anyone got any food?"

Taylor, Quinn and Joy searched their bags and came up with the following;

one small bag of haribo sours

two squashed bananas

one giant bag of Cheetos

“I don’t think Cats should eat Cheetos? Should they?” asked Taylor

“No,” said Quinn decisively, “but we need to make sure he’s ok, you know, for Joe”

Taylor and Joy agreed. So they made a plan to keep the key, and sneak into the shop each day to give him cuddles and cat food, both of which he loved.

And then came the day of the funeral.

The plan was simple but relied on all three being let out of lessons promptly, which meant no ‘not handing their homework in’ or’ not tucking their shirt in’ because the Chapel Havens Funeral Home was a forty-minute walk from school, so there could be no delays.

Also, because they had to fit in feeding Captain America and picking up the flowers that Taylor had taken from his house and hidden in the back room of the store. Taylor completely panicked when he realised that he had no idea how to transport flowers, so he just picked up the entire vase and walked to school with it sloshing around in his bag.

As the final bell approached, each of the Dirtbags started packing their things away, ready to make a quick exit. Joy and Taylor sat together in English, but Quinn was in a different set so was making fast progress towards the changing rooms as they had PE (urgh). This situation made Quinn anxious as getting changed was their most hated experience at school and under normal circumstances Quinn would delay the getting undressed and redressed bit until everyone, or almost everyone, had left the changing rooms. But not today. Quinn knew that they had to get it done quickly because if they didn't meet Taylor and Joy at the blue bins at 3.20 then their entire plan would be ruined.

Quinn made a decision.

They stuffed their school uniform over the top of their PE kit, making them look a little bit like a marshmallow in a blazer, and marched out of the changing rooms, reaching the school gates puffing and sweating at 3.21.

The three of them ran to the store, fed Captain America, grabbed the flowers and headed out to the outskirts of Feckleston-on-the-Wold, to say goodbye to their old friend.

The journey was not quite as straightforward as Taylor had said but thanks to a watery shortcut that Joy found they made it and arrived at 4.02pm.

True to their name, the Dirtbags walked into Chapel Haven Funeral home looking more than a little dishevelled, leaving a little pool of water with each step and carrying a wilting set of three-day-old flowers. Their soggy PE Kits, book bags and backpacks dripped as they stopped outside the door which announced JOSEPH DABROWSKI FUNERAL SERVICE.

"Should we just walk in?" said Taylor, trying to revive the flowers by holding them upside down.

Joy was agitated and hated being late for anything, "Will it have started?" she whispered.

Quinn took a breath. "Remember, we are here to say goodbye to Joe and that's the only thing that matters."

Taylor and Joy nodded and all three held hands.

"Let's open the doors and we'll just sneak in, quietly, at the back, OK?" Quinn was speaking calmly and smiled at them both. "Don't worry."

And so, with their bags and soggy hair and squeaky shoes they quietly turned the handle and opened the double doors into the Chapel of Rest and saw…

No one.

Not a soul.

Not a single other person was there to say goodbye to Old Joe.

All they could see was the casket, surrounded by flowers and resting on a beautiful wooden table, next to it was a picture of a younger and smiling Joe. As they approached the front a lady stepped forward and gave them a leaflet which told them all about which song had been chosen and words that would be said. After a few minutes a kind looking gentleman came out and talked about Joe, making all kinds of references to heroes and superpowers and the three friends smiled at their own memories of this quirky soul. Then the five of them sang 'All Creatures Great and Small' and the casket disappeared through a beautiful velvet curtain. Quinn's shoulders shook again and Taylor and Joy stood quietly with them, trying hard not to think about caskets and curtains but instead superheroes in capes, flying through the sky one last time.

As they went to leave, the kind looking gentleman said, “Can you wait, for just a moment,” and he disappeared into a room at the side of the chapel.

Taylor, Joy and Quinn looked at each other, the flowers still wilting in Taylor’s hands.

Soon, the man returned and approached the three young people who stood before him, soggy and sad.

“I believe,” he said gently, “that this is for you,” and he handed them a battered old shoebox.

Joy took it in her hands and the three of them smiled as they saw, written in big letters:

FOR THE DIRTBAGS.

Five

“Do you think it’s full of money?” said Taylor, looking at the others.

“What?” said Quinn. “Why would it be full of money?”

They all paused.

“Do you think it’s full of … Joe?” said Quinn quietly.

Joy put the shoebox down on the floor and all three took a breath.

Taylor bent down and poked the box. It rattled.

“It’s not Joe,” he said, “Joe didn’t rattle.”

Taylor picked up the box and the three friends sat on a nearby bench and gingerly opened the shoebox.

Inside was a weird collection of items that they recognised as Joe’s favourite things: his grandfather’s WW1 watch, a locket, a completed Rubik’s cube (which he claims to have completed in record time), photos of his family, Captain America’s first collar, old coins from his homeland and a trophy which belonged to his father.

All there, meaningless to many but to these three they meant the world. Quinn picked up the Rubik’s cube and turned it over and over in their hands, trying desperately to conjure up an image of Joe as he told the story sitting at the counter.

“I never believed him,” said Taylor, smiling at the memory

“Yeah, I mean seventeen seconds? That’d be some kind of record,” Joy said, “wouldn’t it?”

"Actually," said Quinn, "the record for completing the Rubik's cube is three point four seven seconds," they smiled for a moment but then tears clouded their eyes, "but I still think Joe was pretty fast."

They placed the Rubik's cube back in the box and Quinn and Joy leafed through the pictures and created names and stories for all of Joe's family. Taylor took out the locket and cleaned it gently with the corner of his shirt, feeling nothing but an emptiness he hadn't known before. Joy picked up the trophy, imagining the sporting triumphs that led to this achievement.

Quinn suddenly spotted a small twenty sided dice, sitting amongst the other treasured items and knew that this was left for him. They grasped it in their hand and briefly brought it to their lips, overcome with sadness.

Eventually the three friends realised it was almost five o'clock. They placed each item carefully in the battered shoebox and as they did, what seemed like a spark flew briefly between each one, throwing light onto The Dirtbags faces as the sky briefly darkened outside the church.

Taylor, Joy and Quinn looked at each other and quickly tucked the box into a backpack and walked briskly home, grateful that the sun was now out to warm their tired bones.

As they passed the shop on their way home, Quinn said, "Just a minute," and dashed off. They returned a few minutes later.

"You OK?" said Taylor, giving his friend a hug.

“Yeah, I just thought,” Quinn’s eyes grew solemn for a moment, “I wanted to keep the shoebox there. For his things to be near him, I guess.”

Taylor nodded and the three of them stood still.

“Also, I thought you might need this,” said Quinn, handing Taylor the vase, who then smirked and tried to stuff it into his bag.

Quinn looked up at the windows of the old man’s flat.

“See you tomorrow, Joe.” they said then raised an eyebrow, a gesture they’d learnt from Joe, and the three Dirtbags headed home.

Six

For the Dirtbags PE was their ABSOLUTE WORST SUBJECT, even worse than Personal, Social thingummy taught by Mr Fistern who found almost everything he had to say acutely embarrassing, especially the presentations which usually led to the entire class having to read something in silence whilst he rearranged his desk drawers.

The reason PE was the absolute worst was not because the Dirtbags hated sport. The reason they hated PE was because of regular and reliable humiliation that accompanied school sport. Not being picked, letting a goal in, getting changed with everyone, coming last, falling down, getting up, getting changed….you get the picture.

There were, in fact, loads of sports that the Dirtbags loved and played on a regular basis, but none of these sports featured in PE. These games had been created by Taylor, Joy and Quinn and were the reason why there was a tally board on the wall of the now empty shop. The main three were:

Dunkin Doughnuts – the aim of the game was to work as a team to spear and devour as many mini doughnuts (bought from Demi's) as possible in three minutes. The 'ringer' threw the ring doughnuts onto the fingers of their teammates. The 'spears' had to splay their hands out and then, if a mini doughnut landed on their finger, eat it in as few bites as possible. Ultimately Dunkin Doughnuts was a battle of accuracy and greed and the current record was fifty-nine doughnuts in three minutes, all of which were consumed by Taylor.

Spitball Archery – this was Quinn's favourite and Joy's worst. Mostly because it involved GROSSNESS. The aim was to get as many small paper balls into the bucket (not THE bucket, obviously, that would be SUPERGROSS) by catapulting them out of your mouth. Quinn was the best because they had a very logical and precise mind, which was also why Quinn was great at Maths and Science. This meant that they had a very clear system when it came to the tearing and balling of the paper, but unfortunately Taylor and Joy never caught sight of Quinn's system because they were too busy wailing as they ripped HUGE sections that couldn't even fit in their mouth. In terms of Spitball Archery Taylor and Joy now knew that trying to beat Quinn was pointless so instead they made bets on how many Quinn would achieve and this resulted in Joy losing her most favourite item EVER, confident that Quinn wouldn't even come close to 100 in a minute BUT what Joy didn't know is that Quinn had been awake till 3am perfecting their now legendary spit and roll technique, and Taylor knew this. Some might call this cheating but Taylor just shrugged. "Don't hate the player, Joy, hate the game,"

Catch 'em or Die – this was a daily challenge for the Dirtbags. It was a simple yet frustrating concept. The three Dirtbags had to keep an item, which could be as simple as a ball or as complex as a hole punch in the air for as long as possible. The rules were:

- The item had to continue to be passed between ALL THREE players
- A maximum break of thirty seconds was allowed (this was challenging if an emergency bucket break was required)

- Every three minutes the key players (Taylor, Joy and Quinn) had to rotate around the room and take one step backwards*

*This was super challenging for Taylor who had a reputation for clumsiness.

Although Catch ‘em or Die was a team sport, it was agreed by the Dirtbags that Joy was often the one who performed some amazing fancy footwork to catch said item which then saved the game from failing and continued the Dirtbags onto their EPIC record which was FIVE HOURS and THIRTEEN MINUTES, achieved one Saturday, surviving four toilet breaks, all by Quinn.

PE was also the worst because it reminded Joy of the Cheerleading Squad Tryouts which had taken place that day. This was a bad day in the secret hideout because despite their best efforts, Taylor and Quinn could not help Joy get over the huge disappointment she felt when, despite having practised for hours, Joy struggled to stay in line and in time. Taylor and Quinn had literally tried everything, including buying all her favourite snacks and dressing Captain America (the cat) up like actual Captain America, which did make her laugh. But it had taken a little bit of joy out of Joy and this made all three of them agree that PE was their absolute worst subject.

So now the Dirtbags were sitting in Old Joe’s, which was their secret hideout. The shop still had the counter and the racks but the place was empty and, although sometimes they used the front room for parkour and Spitball Archery, mostly they hung out in the back room with the old sofa and chair, fridge (which didn’t work but was full of ginger beer) and Captain America’s bed and litter tray (urgh).

School had been tricky for all three of the Dirtbags.

Taylor had had a particularly difficult day, as he walked through the school gates, he spotted Mrs Doobetter lurking and looking and this made Taylor put his head down, fearing the worst. Sure enough, as he approached the school sign that bore the motto ACHIEVING EXCELLENCE EACH DAY (which seemed ironic as the sign was barely hanging on), he heard the sing-song tones of the ever positive and encouraging headteacher. "Tay-ler", she said, then loudly so that everyone stopped and looked at him, "TAY-LER. Have you got a minute?"

Next to Mrs Doobetter was a small child, wearing what looked like brand-new school uniform. Taylor rolled his eyes. He knew what was coming.

"Good morning, Taylor, we've got a brand-new starter this morning. Liam is joining us from the Academy and I wondered if you could give him a little tour of the school? Hmmm?"

Mrs Doobetter tilted her head which meant that you didn't really need to answer.

"I've cleared it with your teachers to miss this morning's lessons. You have double Art."

Taylor let out a very faint sigh as he realised that he not only had to give a school tour, but that he was also going to miss DOUBLE ART which was the only lesson that he truly loved, AND this time he had something really amazing to show his art teacher Mr Fineline, he'd been working on the landscape of Zentropia for over a week, ready for this lesson and now he couldn't even go! Mrs Doobetter was still talking…

"If you can show Liam all the departments, his tutor room, PE changing rooms, where the lockers are and of course the canteen! Yum yum!"

Both Liam and Taylor shared a look at this last bit and the small boy smiled shyly. This made Taylor roll his eyes again and smile back.

"Yeah," he said, "no problem, miss. Come on then." And the unlikely pair set off.

Taylor did take him on the tour of the school BUT he didn't take him to any of the classrooms OR the lockers OR the canteen. Instead, he took Liam to all the best places to hang out, or hide (if that was what you needed to do). He explained who sat where on the field and the playground. He took him to the kitchens where he introduced him to Mr Fields, who would sometimes give you an extra serving of chips or leftover doughnuts if you hung around. He also showed him the clearing in the woods at the back of the school where the Dirtbags hung out during lunch, and Taylor told Liam that if he ever needed somewhere to go, he could come and find him, Quinn and Joy.

“Thanks,” said Liam, “thanks for showing me the hideout. It’s super cool.”

And off Liam went, meaning that Taylor still had twenty minutes left of double art, time enough to show Mr Fineline his new creation, a darker more detailed world within Zentropia and one he hadn’t even shared with Joy and Quinn. Taylor decided to run all the way, and it was worth it.

Taylor left the classroom keen to start his next drawing and spent the next five hours planning, ready for the bell at 3 o’ clock.

Quinn had a tricky day just because. There were days for Quinn where they felt more than usually out of place, more than usually awkward, and this was one of those. Also, Quinn was missing Old Joe. Old Joe had really liked Quinn and Quinn knew it. They felt safe with Old Joe, loved even, and had had some of the best times in their life, sitting around the shop, just the two of them, eating strangely named snacks or crazy delicious treats that Joe had made, and laughing, reading, chatting. Quinn knew they could just be themselves and Old Joe would be happy and this made Quinn’s journey through life a bit easier. So, Quinn missed Joe, some days more than others, and today was just one of those days. They were looking forward to after school when they would see Taylor, Joy and Captain America, of course.

For Joy the day was all about the cheerleading tryouts. Despite having to overcome all her anxieties about just walking into the room, Joy had done it. She'd arrived and, at first, felt OK amongst all the other potential spinners and twisters. She was even given an encouraging smile from Amber, who used to live next door to Joy and was now the head cheerleader on the team.

On the other hand, it was difficult to ignore the voice of Simon Batesfield, one of Joy's least favourite people and the reason she hid by the bins each week.

"Wow, I know we are desperate but this is embarrassing," Simon said loudly as he entered the gym, walking past the line of hopefuls and laughing. "Amber, we should just send them home now?"

"Shut up, Simon," snapped Amber, and Joy smiled a little.

Amber stepped forward and explained that they would all perform the dance routine in groups and that only three people from each group would go forward to Round Two.

Round Two was the one that Joy was looking forward to the most. This involved more jumping and spinning and less counting

Round One started and Joy tried to focus on the beat. She tapped her foot and began to count out loud but out of the corner of her eye saw Simon Batesfield snort and roll his eyes, which made her lose her place and then, before she was even ready, everyone else started the routine. Joy was already behind. She looked to her left and tried to copy the person next to her, but this was Tracy Coppershead who was not fantastic at keeping time, and this confused Joy even more. She could hear the song and knew, from her practice, what should be happening but Tracy wasn't doing the steps that she had learned and Megan and George were both already at the spinning turn and clap section which Joy thought was coming up next. Tears stung Joy's eyes as she realised that she was getting it wrong over and over again, and all she could see was Simon laughing harder and harder.

She heard Simon: "Amber, come on," he protested. "It's embarrassing!"

Amber looked in Joy's direction and gave her a little smile. Joy tried to smile back but didn't have the heart. Instead she just turned and left the gym, her eyes blurred, heading outside to find Taylor and Quinn waiting for her.

Without a word, they handed her a pack of Jelly Smiles, her absolute favourites, and started out of the school gates.

When they reached the shop, instead of doing parkour or reading their favourite comics whilst scoffing snacks at the counter, Taylor immediately took out his sketchbook and sat down on the sofa, deep in thought, and Joy took out her headphones.

So, with their two best friends lost in their own worlds, Quinn wandered over to the counter and traced Old Joe's picture with his finger. The colours were now faded but Taylor had captured the old man's twinkly eyes and this made Quinn smile. Suddenly Captain America joined Quinn, purring like an engine and settling down next to the picture, and Quinn turned to see that Joy was now dancing, in the corner of the room, her face peaceful and happy. She spun and turned to the music and Quinn felt happy to see her smile again.

Quinn turned back to the counter. "I guess it's just you and me then, Captain." They took out their favourite dice. "Wanna play? If I roll a natural twenty then I go to The Snack Shack and buy more Cheetos."

Captain America flipped onto his back, looking for a tummy rub. Quinn obliged.

"But if I roll a six then I have to clean out your litter tray. Urgh."

Old Joe's cat stood up, ready for the game. Usually he would not be allowed near the dice, especially the all hallowed twenty, as this would end with the dice knocked onto the floor, much to Quinn's frustration, but as there was no one else to play with, Quinn accepted his unlikely game partner and got ready to roll.

Just at that point, Joy began to spin round the room, through the racks, round and round, her energy seemed to spark and sparkle through the room and Quinn felt a rush of excitement.

"YES!" shouted Taylor, without warning. "I'm nearly there, Quinn, I'm nearly finished!" and immediately went back to his sketchbook, drawing with a kind of frenetic focus that Quinn had never seen in his good friend before. The room seemed to fizzle with possibilities.

"Maybe," said Quinn to an attentive Captain America, "maybe this will be the time. I'll finally roll a twenty. There's usually only a one in two hundred chance so wish me luck, buddy. Here we go."

Quinn took their dice out from their backpack. Although there were loads of beautiful dice that Quinn had been given by Old Joe, they selected the plainest of them all. White, plastic and worn down through years of use. This had been Joe's favourite and one that he had brought with him all the way from home. It had been in the shoebox that was given to the three friends, and when Quinn found it they knew it had been left for them. From that day on, the dice lived in Quinn's backpack and most days found its way into Quinn's hand, whenever they needed to remind themselves of friendship and kind smiles.

Now it was in Quinn's hand again, ready for the ultimate challenge.

Quinn tipped their hand towards their mouth and whispered the secret magic (this had always made Joe laugh), and gave it the customary shake, back and forth, back and forth. Joy continued to spin and twist, she turned through the air and Quinn thought for a moment they saw traces of light coming from her as she moved faster and faster. Taylor's hand was almost shaking as he created landscapes of vibrant colour, giant fungi sitting amongst luscious, detailed pastures. Their friend was in the zone, building, creating.

Quinn released the battered dice and it quickly skipped over the art covered counter, moving towards Captain America and the shoebox that lived in the corner. Captain America deftly moved his feet and the dice ricocheted off the shoebox and landed right in the middle of Old Joe's face. Quinn caught their breath and took a moment to register the number.

Twenty.

Quinn looked around, astounded. This had never happened!

"Um… Taylor… Joy!" Quinn spoke but no one heard them. Joy was lost now, flying and turning, Taylor's creation began to take shape in front of his eyes.

Quinn rolled again. Twenty.

The room suddenly became dark as the weather outside changed. Clouds of thunder and hard rain spattered the outside of the shop. On the counter, Quinn realised that the shoebox was now full of light, the lid lifting by itself and the pieces inside taking on a life of their own.

Quinn rolled again. Twenty. Again. Twenty.

"Uh… guys… Taylor… Joy…"

The light from the shoebox was now filling the room and suddenly the three friends looked at each other as the floor began to shake.

"What's happening!" shouted Taylor, moving towards Quinn, as the shoebox suddenly lifted from the counter and the watch, trophy, locket, coins, all of Old Joe's most precious things started to rise from the box and travel through the air, in front of their eyes.

Joy looked at her friends, each one of them was glowing. As Taylor moved his hand, he left traces of light, like drawings in the sky. Quinn held the dice which was no longer battered and old but now shimmered with gold and silver flecks.

"Joy, look, look what you can do. You're flying, Joy!"

Joy looked at her feet and realised that she was off the ground. She traced shapes with her shoes and twisted her body round and round, leaving light wherever she went.

And now, in front of the counter, a bright light was forming, the watch and the coins spun towards it. Each of Old Joe's possessions moved into the light, creating a circle which spun and shone, faster and faster, the centre becoming a fiercer and more intense light. As the ground continued to shake, the three friends reached for each other's hands.

"What do we do?" cried Taylor, his voice full of uncertainty and fear.

Quinn looked around, and heard Old Joe's voice. "Trust your instincts. Regret nothing."

Quinn clutched the dice and a shot of light connected them to the portal which was now fully formed, intense and glowing. Taylor smiled at his friend and grabbed the locket. He felt the rush of light run through him, ready to take this journey on.

"Come on, Joy!" he shouted, thinking she was a step behind him but she was already there.

Joy grabbed the trophy and the circle was complete.

Light engulfed the three friends like electricity and as the world around them disappeared they held onto each other tightly.

“Here we go!” Quinn shouted, the noise around them now deafening.

“Oh noooooooooo!” and they held their hands out, the trophy, the dice and locket now glowing as they felt themselves getting pulled in, hurled into a portal of infinite space, travelling through light until

Nothing.

Seven

Joy was flying.

All around her were tiny dots that sparkled as she drew towards them, then seemed to disappear as she passed by. She twisted and turned freely as she hurled through this space that was filled with nothing but light.

Behind her she could hear Taylor and Quinn rushing through the space, calling to her as they all hurtled towards the unknown. Quinn was tumbling, out of control, trying their best to focus on their friends ahead. Taylor was sort of running, his legs moving at a speed he'd never felt before, traces of light still coming from his fingers as he moved them through the tunnel.

Suddenly ahead, a giant ring of intense light appeared and beyond that all they could see was a horizon full of treetops and clouds. The Dirtbags hurtled towards the sky and, before they knew it, they were falling….

Joy shot out from the tunnel of light, turned in the air and landed on both feet in the middle of a blanket of green. Long grasses enveloped her and the surrounding landscape was full of beautiful colours. Joy looked around for her friends but before she could see them, she heard them. First, like a distant cry but soon the noise was coming closer and getting louder until both Taylor and Quinn appeared above her.

Joy stepped out of the way just in time as Quinn tumbled onto the grass around her and Taylor's legs finally stopped moving as he came to a dramatic halt, right in front of Joy's face.

All three friends stopped for a moment, looking at each other and then eventually Joy spoke, “Are we… um, did that just… I mean, I feel like…”

Quinn picked themselves up from the ground and looked around.

“Are you guys OK? That was crazy!”

“I don’t know, I mean, I was running through the air! Was I, is that what happened?!” Taylor looked at his hands then his feet as if to check they were still there.

Joy started laughing, “I was flying, guys, I mean actually flying, like superman or you know actual superwoman!”

“Yes! Joy, you’re totally Superwoman”

“Oh my god”

“THAT WAS AMAZING!!”

“Do you think this is a dream? Like we’ve all fallen into some weird, like coma or something and we are all together in this coma dream thingy” asked Taylor

“What?!?” said Joy and Quinn, together

“Why would we be in a coma, Taylor?” asked Joy to her friend who had begun looking around in wonder.

“I don’t know, like, overdosing on…..Cheetos?”

“We’re not in a coma. Or a dream” said Quinn with a surprising amount of certainty.

“I think..something happened. When we touched Joe’s things, it created, I don’t know, like a portal, or…..” Quinn started to take in their surroundings, "The light, the light was coming from the shoebox and you were both, I mean Joy you were shining and Taylor you were drawing so fast, I've never seen anything like it and then, you know, that light and everything was spinning towards the light."

"A portal? Like…to where?" said Joy, suddenly feeling a little lost and anxious, "Where are we?"

The three friends started to explore their new environment, they walked through towering forests with trees that must have been growing for a thousand years. Sounds echoed above them, movement seemed to be all around them, rustling and shifting through plants that looked familiar but different in a way that they couldn't quite identify. Giant versions of plants that they knew from their own gardens were everywhere but coloured with neon and rainbows, stars and stripes.

"Is this a rainforest?" said Taylor

"Or a jungle?" asked Joy.

Everything was huge, making them feel both protected and intimidated. The came to an opening where large mushroom-like plants sprouted from the earth and formed a sort of staircase which led to an opening in the trees beyond which was a hill.

"Hang on," said Taylor, stopping suddenly, "I know this place."

"Taylor," said Joy, "How can you know this place? We were catapulted through a tunnel of light to get here" She looked around, "This is like nowhere on earth,"

“No,” said Taylor, insistently, “no, I’ve seen this all before. That. There.” He pointed to a giant mushroom. “Well, it’s not a mushroom, it’s a Pyramicus and it’s totally edible and delicious. This is the Village of Life and over there is the jungle habitat and that’s the hills that lead to the…” He tailed off, completely lost for words as he looked around, seeing his own beautiful, detailed creations all around him, larger than life.

“Quinn, Joy, I know where we are. We’ve… I mean I can’t believe it, but somehow we’ve landed in Zentropia.”

“What?” said Quinn and Joy together. “Where?”

“Zentropia,” said Taylor excitedly, “it’s the land, the land I’ve been drawing. The land that started on the counter, at Joe’s but now it’s everywhere. In my sketchbook, on my walls at home. It’s enormous and…” He struggled to find words for a moment. “And… it’s here. It’s where we are standing.”

Quinn moved towards Taylor and looked right into his eyes. They looked around and took in the incredible landscape that his friend had created and then asked, “And… This is quite an important question, Taylor,” said Quinn. “Is Zentropia safe? Are we in danger?”

“Well, every part of it is different. Where we are now everything is green and luscious. All the food is grown here and the animals are born and cared for here. This is the corner of Zentropia that feeds the rest of this world but…” Taylor hesitated, his eyes grew dark and uncertain.

“But?”

“There is another side,” he said, “called Chromicrom which is darker and full of danger.”

“It was after Old Joe died…” His voice faltered. “I just felt a bit… and this world just ended up on the page. I didn’t want to create something so… dark but it just sort of came out and…” Taylor stopped, unable to finish his thought.

Joy took his hand and grabbed Quinn. She smiled.

“This place is beautiful, Taylor. It’s so crazy that we are here!”

Taylor smiled and relaxed. “Oh my god” he said and suddenly rushed over to what looked like a bed of nettles. “These, you can eat these, these are delicious. These are Primbles and they taste like…”

“Cheetos?” said Quinn

“No, not Cheetos. They taste like, whatever you are thinking of, like bananas or ice cream, chips with ketchup or…”

“Cheetos.”

“Well, yeah, OK, Cheetos, if you want.”

Quinn and Taylor dived into the heavy bushes laden with Primbles and started picking off the biggest ones.

Joy looked around. She paused.

“Can we still get home, d’you think?”

Quinn and Taylor turned to look at her.

“Why are we here?”

Quinn walked over to Joy and gave her a quick hug. “I don’t know,” they mumbled through a mouthful of food.

“We must be here for a reason, can’t just be for the Primbles.” Said Quinn. Taylor and Joy smiled.

“So let’s find the reason.” Quinn looked into their worried faces, trying to see if this was OK, if they would join them on this adventure.

“I think we should go towards that hill,” said Taylor, “don’t ask me why.”

“OK,” said Joy, “let’s go towards that hill and see what happens.”

But before they could set off, a voice seemed to come from the sky behind them, loud and booming. In the distance music played and chanting could be heard and then the voice again, a voice that they almost recognised announced,

“THE TOURNAMENT IS ABOUT TO BEGIN. WILL THE DIRTBAGS PLEASE COME TO THE STADIUM!”

Eight

As Taylor, Quinn and Joy approached the stadium, the noise was almost deafening. Speakers the size of houses sat either side of a giant structure which glistened and gleamed in the sun. Music blared out and the sound of the crowd leapt over the sides of the building and crashed all around the three friends.

“Taylor!” hissed Joy. “You never said you created a stadium!”

Taylor looked bewildered. “I… I… didn’t. This isn’t part of Zentropia. I never drew this!”

“Maybe this is Joe?” said Quinn.

“Why would Joe do this, call us to a STADIUM? WHERE SPORT HAPPENS?” Joy was agitated and nervous.

The voice came over the speakers once again: "THE TOURNAMENT IS ABOUT THE BEGIN. WILL THE DIRTBAGS PLEASE COME TO THE STADIUM!"

And that's when they heard it. The chanting from the crowd: "Dirtbags… Dirtbags… DIRTBAGS!"

Over and over again.

The three of them moved instinctively towards the sound and gasped as a halo of light opened up and beckoned them onwards, into the tunnel and the enormous stadium which was alive with colour and movement.

The sound of the crowd was incredible, as they entered the arena a huge wave of cheers erupted from the stands around them. People rushed to the barriers and called their names as the Dirtbags looked around, confused and bewildered.

"Taylor, over here!"

"Joy, you are amazing!"

"We love you, Quinn!"

Taylor, Joy and Quinn couldn't believe what they were seeing, everywhere there were rows of people, chanting their names, leaning forward to get a glimpse of the famous Dirtbags.

"What are we doing here?" said Joy.

Suddenly an announcement was made and the entire stadium went silent.

"WELCOME TO THE FINALS OF THE GRAND ZENTROPIAN TOURNAMENT. WE ARE DELIGHTED

TO BE HOSTING THIS YEAR'S EVENT HERE AT THE STADIUM OF THE GODS. THIS YEAR WE WELCOME BACK LAST YEAR'S WINNERS, THE MAVERICKS, AND FRESH FROM THEIR INCREDIBLE JOURNEY … IT'S THE DIRTBAGS!"

The crowd went wild and flags and banners sprung up all around the stadium, emblazoned with The Dirtbags logo, complete with Captain America in team colours. The chant began again: "Dirtbags… Dirtbags… DIRTBAGS!"

In the distance, Joy spotted the other team's supporters, all dressed in gold and beside them a huge eagle.

"Look," she said, "the other team, they've got a mascot!"

"We don't have a mascot," said Quinn who suddenly thought they might need to use the emergency bucket, "what do we do?"

Before they had a chance to make a decision, two people ushered them towards a small doorway underneath the seating stands. As they approached the stands a small girl rushed forward and leaned over the railings waving and shouting.

"Joy, I love you, you're the best!"

Joy smiled at the little girl and said thanks, even though she didn't understand why. As she turned towards the door, she heard the familiar refrain of a cheerleading chorus and stopped to watch the perfectly performed routine. Her smile faded, just for a moment but then Taylor leaned forward and took her hand.

"Come on, Joy," he said as they were joined by an excited young woman dressed head to toe in the tournament's official logo and colours. She bounded over to them and shook their hands.

"Taylor, Joy, Quinn, we are delighted that you could make it. So fantastic to have you here."

The three friends looked confused but then Taylor stepped forward.

"Thanks, it's excellent to be here." He smirked at his two friends. "Can you show us to our changing room please? We'd like to prepare for the tournament."

The official burst into action, delighted to be able to help. "Of course, of course" she said, "I'm sure you'd like to check your equipment for Round One and get changed. It's right this way." And she gestured towards a large impressive-looking door which stated:

The Dirtbags' Changing Room

DO NOT ENTER

As they wandered towards the door, Quinn asked, "What is Round One? You know, just, you know, checking…"

"The first round is Rings of Destiny. As you know, it's where the contestants have to launch giant cannonballs into the arena using only the slingshot and their own strength and wit. We've prepared your equipment and it's ready for inspection in the arena. But first I'm sure you'd like to change into your kit and ready yourselves for the battle of a lifetime!"

This last bit was said like an announcement on the telly and made the Dirtbags smile awkwardly as the official shook their hands and left them to prepare. The official stuck her head round the door once more.

“Good luck!” she said. “I’m not supposed to say it but I really want you to win! Go, Dirtbags!”

The door shut behind her and the Dirtbags all stood still, taking in their surroundings and the challenge before them. Joy started pacing the room, Taylor sat quietly in the corner and Quinn stood nervously by the door, every now and then peeking out to see if someone was coming to get them. Quinn spoke first.

“Oh my god,” they said, “any minute now, without warning, someone is going to walk in here and expect us to go out there –” Quinn pointed to the huge arena, which was now alive with music and chanting. “Go out there and play… what was it?” Their mind seemed to have gone completely blank in all the confusion and excitement.

“Rings of Destiny,” said Taylor, without looking up.

“Right, Destiny, right,” Quinn confirmed, nodding their head.

“But, I mean, if this is the final, when were all the other, you know, tournaments, and how were we there…?” Joy continued to pace as the reality of their situation hit her. “Is this a dream?”

“And if this is Round One, what happens next? I mean, I can’t play,” said Taylor. “You can’t play, I mean, none of us, none of us should be here. We haven’t even got proper tracksuits or anything.”

Just then a small man opened the door and entered the room silently, like a ninja, except that instead of nunchucks, he was carrying a set of tracksuits.

"Your official kit has arrived," he said and placed the brightly coloured clothes down on the table in the centre of the room.

The Dirtbags looked at each other then looked at him. The ninja with the sportswear.

Then he left, as silently as he had entered, and the three friends approached the table.

"Well, I guess these are mine," said Taylor, picking up a T-shirt which had his name and his face all over it. "Oh god." He sighed. "It's like Let's Learn all over again."

"At least you can see your face!" exclaimed Joy, turning her T-shirt over to discover an image of her flying through the air like a blur.

"And look at me," Quinn said, holding theirs up for Taylor and Joy to see. On the back was a picture of Quinn scowling, with one eyebrow raised, like a trademark.

"So," said Joy, "we'll put these on and then we'll walk out into that arena, yes?"

"Yes," agreed Taylor with a confidence he didn't feel, "and we'll go play Rings of Destiny, right, Quinn?"

But Quinn wasn't listening. They had been reminded of the horrors of PE, having to change as rapidly and silently as possible. Joy looked at their face, knowing the discomfort that was going on inside.

“Don’t worry, Quinn,” she said, “it’s just us. And we’ve seen you use the Emergency Bucket so…”

All three of them laughed and then changed into their bright and shiny new kit, emblazoned with *Go, Dirtbags!* on the front, neon stripes down the side and awkward pictures on the back.

Just then the excited-looking official knocked on the door and asked if they were ready.

“Are we?” said Taylor.

“I don’t feel ready,” said Joy.

Quinn looked towards the door and put their hands in their pockets. Suddenly they felt something small in the palm of their hand, they closed their fist and brought their hand out to see what it held. To Quinn’s astonishment it was the twenty-sided dice, battered and old but there, reminding them all of the journey that had already completed and the adventure to come.

“We’re READY!” Quinn said, loudly and turned to their friends.

“Come on. COME ON. We might not know what we are about to do but we are READY!”

“Ready for what though, Quinn?” said Taylor, looking at his best friend.

“Who knows, but we spend our whole lives ready to fight, to protect ourselves, to protect each other. We plan every day, every moment, ready for something or someone to make life hard. So we are READY. Ready for anything, OK?”

The crowd began to chant again: “Go, dirtbags… Go, Dirtbags… GO, DIRTBAGS!”

The three friends walked out of the door and into the arena, cameras flashed and the crowd went wild.

Nine

As they entered the stadium, Taylor, Joy and Quinn couldn't believe what they were seeing. The stadium was packed, every seat taken and the red, blue and shining gold that adorned their kit was mirrored throughout the stands. People waved flags emblazoned with the Dirtbags logo, kids with T-shirts just like their own waved and cheered and in the distance a band began to play. Quinn took in the surroundings. The stadium was enormous, giant screens sat atop each corner and the whole thing was surrounded by majestic trees and plant life. Wild birds dipped in and out of the leaves and added to a cacophony of sound that was hard to imagine. Cameras whizzed around the perimeter of the arena, capturing the atmosphere and every now and again someone would see their face pop up on the giant screen and a tiny part of the crowd around them would go crazy. A mexican wave drove its way through the stands and the band started playing the Dirtbags' favourite song.

Joy looked around and couldn't believe what she was seeing, people calling her name, T-shirts and flags showed her flying through the air and in the distance she heard the cheerleaders start:

"Give me a D!"

"D!"

"Give me an I!"

Joy couldn't stop smiling and she waved, looking round at all these people, these people who seem to love her.

Quinn was feeling overwhelmed, the noise of the stadium, the flashing lights and people everywhere suddenly made them feel totally lost, unable to see the task ahead. Just then Quinn looked up and saw an entire row of people dressed up as Cheetos! They rubbed their eyes to be sure they weren't hallucinating but there they were, a whole row of people dressed as giant orange bags of cheesy awesomeness. They jostled and laughed and every now and again the middle one would get squished and a whole load of orange dust would erupt from his bag and cover the row in front, who laughed and then licked their faces and fingers.

Whilst Quinn and Joy were taking in the whole experience, Taylor was looking off into the distance, into the hills beyond the stadium and the dark clouds that rose above them. The clouds of Chromicron. Taylor thought about how he had felt when he created that world and wondered what it would mean for the three of them once this new adventure was over but before he could disappear into his own dark thoughts, a small boy ran over and tugged on his shirt.

"Taylor," he said, "Taylor. Will you sign my sketchbook? You're the best!"

He looked up at Taylor and handed him his sketchbook.

"I drew Captain America for you, but it's not very good," he said, looking at the ground.

Taylor took the sketchbook and bent down to talk to the boy.

He looked at the sketch and smiled, "Hey, look, you've got his eyes just right and here, the way he crossed his paws. Perfect. Just keep going, keep drawing!"

Taylor signed the sketchbook and handed it back to the boy, who was now smiling back at him in wonder.

"Thanks, Taylor, you're my favourite." And he ran back to his parents, shouting, "GO, DIRTBAGS!"

Over on the other side of the stadium, the Dirtbags watched as the rival team entered the space, accompanied by a banner-waving entourage. As they strode in, the band hammered out a new tune.

"Wow!" said Joy. "They've got entrance music!"

"Yeah," said Taylor, "and there are LOADS of them! LOOK!"

The Dirtbags' eyes went wide as three teammates entered followed by an army of trainers and supporters, all dressed in beautifully detailed tracksuits, each one embroidered with their mascot, a regal and glorious eagle.

Quinn gulped and reached into their pocket to find the dice. Joy hopped from foot to foot and Taylor stuffed his hands into pockets.

Joy traced patterns in the sandy floor with her foot.

"Maybe the rest are family and friends?" mumbled Quinn, looking around for some sign that everything was going to be OK.

"Come on, you two," said Taylor, "come on. We are the Dirtbags!"

Taylor looked around him and waved, the crowd went wild and a chant erupted from the stands:

"Dirtbags, Dirtbags, DIRTBAGS!"

"YEAH!" said Joy, waving both her arms madly at the crowd and spinning on the spot, driving them crazy. "WE ARE THE DIRTBAGS!"

"DIRTBAGS! DIRTBAGS! DIRTBAGS!"

The chant got louder and louder and louder until a booming voice came over the speakers and the giant screens focused on the official who stood in front of the Dirtbags, commanding the attention of the crowd.

"WELCOME, WELCOME TO YOU ALL AND THANK YOU FOR COMING ALONG TO THE FINAL OF THE GRAND ZENTROPIAN TOURNAMENT SET IN THE HEART OF THE ZENTROPICS. IN JUST A FEW MINUTES THE TOURNAMENT WILL GET UNDERWAY WITH BOTH TEAMS TAKING PART IN ROUND ONE.

WILL ANYONE REACH THE GOLDEN MARKER AND TAKE THE TITLE OR WILL BOTH TEAMS BE FORCED TO BATTLE IT OUT TO THE END?

WE WILL SEE!

FIRST EACH TEAM MUST SELECT THE ORDER IN WHICH THEY WILL COMPETE AND THEN THEY WILL HAVE FIVE MINUTES TO PREPARE THEIR EQUIPMENT AND GET INTO POSITION."

The Dirtbags felt like they were in a dream, everywhere cameras were going off and suddenly their faces were transmitted on the giant screens, high atop the stadium walls. Taylor quickly ran his fingers through his hair, Joy couldn't stop smiling and Quinn delighted the crowd as they gave their signature move.

As the crowd continued to go wild, music started up and the super-keen official who had showed them to their changing room darted over.

"We are ready for you over in the arena," she said, catching her breath. Then, realising that she was also now pictured on the giant screens, the official waved enthusiastically and screamed, "GO, DIRTBAGS!" Just as quickly realising that she shouldn't have said that, she backed out of the picture.

"Your slingshot has arrived and been prepared independently but I'm sure you'd like to make the final adjustments?" She looked expectantly at the three friends who paused for a moment, wondering what they were meant to do but then said, "Yes… absolutely…right, yeah… let's do it." They followed her across the track and field area onto a huge white painted circle. At the edge of the circle and scattered along the coloured lines were red, yellow and green numbers, and in the centre was a small but shiny gold sphere that caught the light from every angle, blinding the Dirtbags as they travelled towards it.

"That's the golden marker," said the official, who was proving to be invaluable as she was keen to share her knowledge of every element of the games with The Dirtbags, even though they were meant to know it already.

Her name was Sally. "If you hit it then you win the round outright, well I mean you know that don't you. There's one in every game, you know, but no one ever hits it."

"No one?" said Quinn incredulously.

“What, ever?” said Joy, looking at Taylor, who was frowning.

“No,” said Sally, “apparently it’s pretty much impossible. The angles surrounding the golden marker make it so hard to hit that no one’s ever done it.” She nodded wisely and led them over to where theIr slingshot was sitting, ready for action.

The Dirtbags stopped in their tracks as they saw the slingshot for the first time. It was enormous. Taller than Taylor, who was the tallest Dirtbag, taller than Taylor’s dad, who was six feet, two inches, and probably as tall as all three Dirtbags put together. It had the Dirtbag logo emblazoned on each side and the whole thing was painted gold. The sling was black and shiny and hung down like a giant hammock, ready to be stretched and swung in this first epic battle.

Taylor, Joy and Quinn all looked at each other and then moved silently around the beautiful and intimidating structure. They glanced across the arena to see their rival team, inspecting their equally sized and especially shiny slingshot. The Mavericks appeared to be taking measurements and adjusting things, so the Dirtbags started to do the same, moving around the slingshot, randomly measuring things with their fingers and saying, in loud voices,

“Excellent!”

“Yes, good.”

“Ah, this needs tightening,” said Quinn unexpectedly and the other two Dirtbags looked at them but Quinn just shrugged.

“What are you doing?” asked Joy quietly as she moved around the sling.

"Pretending," hissed Quinn. "We need to look like we know what we are doing, especially now!"

"Why now?" said Taylor, looking around, but no sooner had he said it then he realised what Quinn was talking about.

Striding in formation across the painted arena were the Mavericks, like a pack of animals or wild birds approaching their prey and then, in one swift movement, each member put sunglasses on without breaking step.

"Huh," said Joy, trying not to be entirely impressed by their ability to coordinate brain and body. "Who needs sunglasses anyway?" she said, looking at her teammates.

Just then the sun emerged from the clouds and bright light streamed into the stadium, blinding the stands and drenching the arena in sunlight.

"We do," said Quinn, squinting into the sky.

As the rivals reached each other, the leader of the team approached Taylor with his arm outstretched Quick as a flash Joy stepped forward, "Hi," she said, "I'm Joy, and this is my team, the Dirtbags." She shook his hand and he lowered his glasses.

"Good luck," said the leader of the Mavericks, who had introduced himself as Catcher Day. "May the best team win." He lowered his glasses once more and looked directly at Joy. "See you out there." And then clicking his fingers he turned on his heels, and the rest of his team followed, making their way back to their side of the arena as the band played their song.

As soon as the Mavericks turned to leave the Dirtbags all sat down in the sling which acted like a giant swing and rocked them gently in the warm air.

“Well, this is it then, I guess,” said Taylor, “almost time.”

But Joy couldn’t hear him. All she was thinking about was Simon Batesfield and the cheerleading tryouts. The leader of the Mavericks had even given her that look that made her want to squidge herself behind the bin again, but she was brought back to the arena by Quinn.

“Joy… JOY!” said Quinn. “How big do you think they’ll be?” Taylor and Quinn both looked at her.

Joy looked confused. “How big will what be?” she asked.

“The shot,” Taylor and Quinn spoke together.

“If this is the sling… how big is the shot?” said Quinn, reaching for the dice.

Joy squinted into the sun and stood, as the announcement came over the speaker.

“HERE WE GO….RINGS OF DESTINY!!”

“I think we are about to find out,” she said.

Ten

No sooner had she said those words than a fanfare boomed across the stadium and the giant screens whirred into life playing footage from previous tournaments and messages from Zentropian champions. To the Dirtbags it seemed like the weather changed, the wind whipped up and the sky grew ominous. Taylor, Joy and Quinn stood awestruck then turned as they heard a rumbling noise that came from behind them.

“What’s that?” said Quinn.

Joy looked around. “I think we know what the shots are now,” she said as a number of what looked like huge globes of steel were lined up by tournament officials next to the Dirtbags’ slingshot.

There were eight of the globes in total and the contestants were to use each one to try and gain as many points as possible by hurling them into the scoring circle.

Scoring for Cannonball Slingshot looked like this:

Red marker = thirty points

Yellow marker = fifty points

Green marker = eighty points

GOLD MARKER = TOTAL VICTORY!

“Who goes first?” said Taylor.

“Oh, that’s easy,” said Sally, who had taken it upon herself to become the Dirtbags’ unofficial official, “why don’t you do it the same as you do at every tournament?”

"Right, yeah, exactly," said Quinn, "so it's me, Taylor, then Joy?"

Sally looked round and raised her eyebrow at Quinn. At first Quinn thought she was mocking them but then Sally smiled and said, "Oh, I see, this is like a test…? How well do I know the Dirtbags?"

The Dirtbags laughed awkwardly and stayed silent, waiting for the answer.

"Well, obviously, Quinn, you do this round because you are the best at Slingshot, then Taylor in the second event for Rings of Fire and then Joy for the third, because, you know, duh." Sally elbowed Taylor and rolled her eyes. "Obviously."

"Yeah," said Quinn, "obviously."

They looked at Taylor and Joy, both of whom shrugged.

"Right then," said Quinn, "I'm first," and walked over to the shiny spheres to inspect them.

"Hey, Joy, Taylor, these aren't heavy at all!" Quinn spoke in hushed tones, looking around for the ever keen Sally. The two friends joined them and all three of them moved the shots around. They were actually made of some sort of woven material which was incredibly light.

"So, all you have to do," said Taylor, "is use the slingshot to throw this ball into that space and hit one of those markers?"

"Yep," said Joy, "Like archery? Quinn, it's like Spitball Archery!"

Quinn's face lit up for a moment and then remembered the task ahead

“Maybe the Mavericks go first?” they said quietly

“Don’t worry,” said Sally walking over to them, “the Mavericks go first.”

Just then another fanfare sounded and a voice came over the system:

“ARE YOU READY FOR CANNONBALL SLINGSHOT?”

The stadium erupted with sound and light, flags were waved and streamers appeared from the sky, covering the ground in every colour imaginable.

This was it.

Quinn stepped up onto the platform and watched as the Maverick contestant placed their first shot within the sling, aiming towards the outer scoring ring, for the highest points. As they pulled the sling into place the crowd cheered and drummed their feet on the stands and everyone seemed to hold their breath.

WHOOSH!

The Maverick let go of the slingshot and the whole crowd watched as the agile ball arched its way through the sky, over the golden marker, and came to land in the middle of the non-scoring zone.

The entire stadium let out a groan but then almost immediately after came huge cheers as the second shot seared through the air and smacked down on a red marker! Thirty points!

The Maverick player wasted no time in using all eight shots, racking up a total of 260 points. This might seem like a lot to the Dirtbags but judging by the scowl on Catcher Day's face it wasn't great.

So now it was Quinn's turn.

Quinn watched as the Maverick player stepped down from the platform, head hung low, and they felt a pang of sympathy for them. Taylor and Joy stood at the bottom of the slingshot and at their friend.

"Come on, Quinn, you can do it," said Taylor but Quinn was staring off into the distance, concentrating intently on the scoring circle and talking quietly to themselves.

Quinn stepped up onto the giant slingshot, took a deep breath and steadied themself. At that moment, the band struck up, playing their favourite song in the world, and the crowd responded by letting out a huge chant. "GOOOOOOOOO, DIRTBAGS!"

Quinn smiled awkwardly as they heard people call their name and reached down, picked up their first shot and felt the woven material. It was so much lighter than previously thought, they turned it around in the light, lifting it up and down, studying it from every angle.

"You can do it," they said to themselves. "Come on, Quinn. Eighty points." They repeated, "Eighty points." Quinn eyed the green marker on the far side of the scoring circle.

"Quinn, Quinn, QUINN!"

They looked down and Taylor and Joy had joined in the chant. Then a voice came over the speakers: "SILENCE, PLEASE."

The entire crowd fell into hushed silence, expectant, waiting for Quinn to make their first move.

Quinn placed the shot inside the sling and took hold of two large handles. Quinn's hands were small yet seemed to fit inside the handles perfectly, like it was made for them.

"Come on, Quinn, you've got this," said Taylor softly.

Quinn took in a huge breath and, using all their strength, pulled back the thick black sling as far as it could go. They anchored themself in the sandy ground, digging their heels and arching their back. They knew where they were heading. They visualised the green marker, then counted to three:

"Three… Two… One!" And they released the sling.

The giant shot launched into the air, going way over the heads of their two teammates who let out a huge, "WOAH!" Quinn ran onto the top of the platform to see where it landed. It was travelling fast, flying through the sky, past the red marker and going, still rising, the giant sphere was not yet falling to the ground.

"Go on," said Quinn, under their breath.

"GO ON!" called Sally, the official, and then looked round, suddenly remembering that she should support both teams.

The crowd let out a huge cheer as the sphere started its descent and then started drumming their feet on the floor.

It flew past the yellow marker now and was hurtling towards the green line, but would it hit the marker?

Quinn was suddenly aware that the odds of this happening were really small. They turned away, prepared to hear the groan from the audience but suddenly all around them were green streamers and the giant screens whirred into life as Quinn turned and saw their shot land.

THWACK!

Right in the centre of the green marker.

"EIGHTY POINTS!" screamed the announcer and the crowd joined them in celebrating and congratulating Quinn.

"EIGHTY POINTS TO THE DIRTBAGS! WILL QUINN TAKE THE LEAD IN CANNONBALL SLINGSHOT?" came the voice over the speakers.

Quinn smiled, wide-eyed, amazed at this new victory.

But the game was not won yet, and Quinn knew it. They still had another seven shots to go and, having watched their preceding competitor, they understood that this could just be beginner's luck.

They took another breath and picked up their second shot.

Their second shot lined up, Quinn took a step back and dug their heels in as before, but on this occasion as they let go one of their feet became dislodged and the shot careered off into the distance, away from the green marker. Quinn knew their chances of scoring now were limited. They watched as their second shot disappeared into the distance and was deemed to be out of the scoring zone.

"Focus," they said, to themself and then turned to Taylor and Joy mouthing, "Sorry."

They both shook their heads.

"No," said Taylor, "don't be silly. You are doing amazing."

"Yeah," said Joy, "you've already got eighty points, you don't need much more. You can do it!"

"Thanks," Quinn said, trying to seem confident. They didn't quite believe their friends, especially as Taylor's hands were firmly in his pockets and Joy looked like she needed to use the emergency bucket.

However, they dug in for the third shot, again thinking about the green marker, aiming for the highest points, and then letting it fly.

The crowd were with them, clapping and drumming their feet. They saw the Mavericks on the other side, using binoculars to track the shot's progress. They looked over and Catcher Day gave Quinn a tiny salute and a wry smile.

"Where have I seen him before?" thought Quinn.

But there was no time for that, Quinn's second shot scored, but only thirty points, and the next one landed nowhere near the markers.

Four left. Still on 110. 150 to go.

"Come on, Quinn, come on, Quinn," they thought to themself but the fifth shot careered off into the no scoring zone.

Quick as a flash, Quinn picked up their sixth shot and reloaded. They breathed deeply and thought back to the feeling they had when they were in the portal, flying, weightless. Quinn reached into their pocket and felt the dice, they turned it over and over between their fingers. Hands back in the sling Quinn pictured Joe's face, and as they exhaled they let the sling go, visualising the shot working its way through the sky, hurtling towards the green line.

They looked up. The shot was high in the air, passing the golden marker, and suddenly Quinn realised that it was too high, it was set to go way past the green marker, beyond the scoring zone.

Just then a wild wind whipped up and flew through the stadium, Quinn watched as their shot swerved to the left then to the right and then began its descent. To their amazement, Quinn realised that the shot was now heading back towards the green marker.

"God," said Quinn, "this could be it!"

Down it fell, whipped by a wind which swirled and whirled around them all, making Taylor groan about the state of his hair and Quinn's Cheetos fans disappear in the cloud of orange dust.

But the shot was still firmly on its way to earning the Dirtbags eighty points.

"Come on," said Taylor, Joy and Sally, "COME ON!" they shouted.

THWACK!

Down it came, making its mark in the scoring circle. Then the crowd let out a giant "OOOOOOO" and Quinn watched as people around the stadium started pointing and talking and each of the Mavericks got out their binoculars and trained them on their last shot.

“What’s going on?” said Quinn to Sally, who was hopping from foot to foot.

She looked up at Quinn and then spoke to all three of them, “It means that it’s not quite on the marker, so it’s not in the centre. So what happens now is that the official has to go and inspect it, well, you know, the official official, the top one. They will make a decision on whether it scores or not.” Sally went back to scrutinising the shenanigans surrounding Quinn’s shot and biting her nails.

“Right, OK.”

“So there’s a certain percentage that they’re looking for. It can’t just be on there a little bit. It must be over 47.8% touching the green marker or it’s no good. I always said it’s completely unfair but no one listens to me.”

“Right, so there’s a chance?” said Joy

“It was a really good shot,” said Taylor, nodding.

“There’s definitely a chance,” said Quinn, smiling at them both.

The official official stood in front of the shot with a large tape in hand. Two other people known as the checkers came over and, well, checked that everything was correct and above board and all the cameras were directed at the action around Quinn’s shot.

Moments later, the checkers left the circle, followed by the official official, and soon a little huddle formed over by the stadium entrance. Quinn climbed down from the platform and stood with their two friends. Suddenly the cameras swung round to focus on the Dirtbags as the announcement came:

"A DECISION HAS BEEN MADE..."

The entire stadium was silent. The Dirtbags held their breath.

"NO SCORE!"

A huge groan erupted from the crowd and from Quinn. With just two shots left, Quinn was on 110 points and needed at least another 150 to beat the Maverick player who had come before them. Problem was, they had already hit both green markers, so these were out of action, and there was no way to get another eighty. With only two shots left to go there was no way to get more than a 100 and, at this point, this felt like an impossible task to Quinn.

"Right," Joy said, "go for the fifty, Quinn, go for the yellow. Just get as many points as you can at this stage. Whatever you manage will help us in the next round!"

The yellow markers were slightly larger than the green and there were a few more of them. The red were larger and more plentiful still, littered around the circle. But Quinn wasn't listening. Instead they were standing totally still, looking out onto the field in front of them, eyes moving from green to yellow to red, and finally landing on the golden marker.

The golden marker was no bigger than a dinner plate, with what seemed like a dip in the centre. The ground surrounding it looked dented and uneven, rough patches of grass sprouting here and there, making it even harder to see.

The crowd waited.

Quinn started to talk quietly to themselves, and as they moved past Joy and Taylor, they heard them whisper, "...be aware of the wind. It's now whipping it round to the right but you can use that to your advantage. Think about where you're placing your shot…"

The crowd began to call out, as Quinn headed into the scoring circle, walking slowly and every now and then stopping to look back to the Dirtbags' platform.

"I don't know if they are allowed to do that," said Sally, looking at Joy and Taylor, both of whom were now looking at each other, concerned for their friend.

The official officials started another huddle in the corner of the arena and the Mavericks stood heckling and throwing their hands around in protest

Quinn stood in the centre, their feet touching the golden marker, unaware that the stadium was hanging on their every move.

"What is Quinn doing?" said Joy, to Taylor who was now watching as Quinn started pointing and moving his arms around, looking up into the sky then down to the marker which was below him.

"Trig," said Taylor, smiling, "he's doing Trigonometry! Like in Spitball Archery! Joy! He's going for the golden marker." By this point Taylor was whispering and pulling Joy off to the side so no one could hear them.

"Joy, you know how Quinn is super smart?"

"Yeah."

"And completely kills it in maths…"

"Yeah."

"And is always talking to us about angles and momentum and stuff?"

"Yeah, YES, Taylor, what are you saying?"

"Well, they are doing it now, they are using all of that to work out how to hit the golden marker. I just know they are!"

Just then, as if from nowhere, Sally appeared next to them, making them jump. She was carrying a huge red folder marked *Rules and Regulations*.

"No," she said, "I was wrong. There's absolutely nothing in here that says Quinn cannot enter the scoring circle. So if they try to disqualify them, I'll be ready." And she strode towards the edge of the circle, folder in hand.

Quinn stood, then started their way back to the platform to take their final shot. As Quinn approached them Taylor and Joy both nodded and in a moment of divine synchronicity, all three Dirtbags high-fived.

"This is the coolest I've ever been," said Taylor excitedly, looking round for Joy but she had followed Quinn towards the platform and the two of them were now in a huddle at the bottom of the steps.

Taylor rushed over.

"But how do you know?" asked Joy in a hushed voice

"I don't," replied Quinn, "I'm just going to trust my instinct. Remember, like Joe said."

Joy looked concerned and started hopping from one foot to the other.

“Look,” said Quinn, “the truth of the matter is that, well, we can never really know how things are going to turn out. We can’t predict the future.”

“That would be cool.”

“Yeah, Taylor, I know, but we just have to do our best and trust Joe, trust what he told us. This is my decision. To go for the golden marker. Do you trust me?” Quinn asked, looking at their two best friends.

Taylor and Joy nodded, then all three of them smiled and did the Dirtbags handshake which made the crowd go crazy.

Quinn looked up at the fans and then started to climb the steps onto the platform. As they reached the top stood for a moment and visualised the golden marker. Eyes closed, Quinn started seeing the arena, numbers and symbols spinning into place, flight paths in neon and gold appeared before them. Quinn took a deep breath and picked up their next shot. They turned it over and over in their hands with a concentrated look on their face. Over and over, hand to mouth, over and over.

Then.

Breath. Hands. Handles.

“What are you doing?” hissed Sally from beneath the platform. “Quinn, no one has EVER hit the golden marker. As your unofficial official I suggest you go for the highest score available. Go for the yellow!”

But Quinn wasn’t listening. They made tiny adjustments and, instead of aiming at the sky, they angled it towards the ground.

The Mavericks crowded onto the front of their platform, pushing for space to see what Quinn was doing.

Quinn stood for a moment and then pulled back the sling, halfway. One final adjustment and then

they pulled back and BOOM! The shot flew from the sling moving into the scoring circle but quickly descended and landed on the grassy surface where it kept rolling, the momentum pushing it forward, making slow progress, inching its way towards the golden marker.

There was an audible gasp from the stands as everyone suddenly realised what Quinn was trying to do and beneath him Taylor, Joy and Sally held their breath. Taylor reached for Joy's hand and squeezed it tight.

Quinn watched as the shot continued its journey, moving over the uneven ground, following the twists and turns until it approached the centre point.

The shot was now moving incredibly slowly and for a moment it skirted the edge of the golden marker.

A huge cheer erupted from the crowd, but Quinn closed their eyes knowing that it had yet to reach its final resting place.

"47.8%," Quinn whispered to themselves and reached into their pockets just as a groan came from beneath the platform. The shot moved off the golden marker and for a moment Taylor and Joy lowered their heads, afraid to watch, sure that Quinn's final shot had missed its mark.

But the shot was still moving and Quinn was now leaning forward, over the edge of the platform, concentrating and whispering as he traced its progress into the dips and dents that surrounded the shining sphere.

It seemed like the shot had come to a stop. It was barely moving and the giant screens showed the entire stadium that it was just about resting on the edge of the circle, teasing the crowd with the possibility of witnessing the first ever golden marker score. The cameras zoomed in on Quinn's face, their lips were moving, willing the shot to make its move. In their mind, Quinn continued to see a map of directional arrows, numbers and patterns, they took the dice from their pocket and brought them up to their face, speaking in riddles, hoping for this act of destiny to take place.

As Quinn closed their eyes, a wind arrived in the arena and whipped through the stands, like a Mexican wave, tornado-like, ruffling the Mavericks as they stood and waited, making its way inwards, towards the centre, until it seemed to find the shot that sat poised on the edge of glory.

Quinn opened their eyes and watched open mouthed as the final shot tipped, as if in slow motion, and turned itself over, coming to rest at the heart of the golden marker.

Suddenly, the sky was filled with light as beams of pure gold shot from all around the stadium and streamers of gold paper seemed to come from nowhere, surrounding Quinn and the platform where they stood, dumbfounded, silent, until Taylor and Joy were by their side, jumping and hugging each other and Quinn in a moment of pure unbelieving excitement.

As the noise and commotion grew around them, Quinn put their hand in their pocket and drew out the battered dice. They raised it to their lips and looked up into the sky, "Thanks, Joe," said Quinn softly to themselves, but Taylor and Joy heard them and stepped forward, joining hands, and the Dirtbags stood together at the heart of this carnival of gold, heads dipped low, remembering their quirky old friend.

As the cheers died down and the sky cleared, the announcements confirmed that Round One was now complete, the Dirtbags had done it! Quinn had hit the golden marker which automatically defeated the Mavericks, who were now huddled together at the bottom of the platform. Catcher Day was standing in the centre, hands on hips, looking across the field at the Dirtbags, as if he was trying to challenge them, but the Dirtbags were busy.

"Oh my god, Quinn," said Taylor with excitement, "oh my god……OH MY GOD!"

Quinn laughed at their friend, who was now speaking so quickly that he made no sense at all, and Joy joined them, finally catching hold of Taylor and saying, "Slow down, Taylor, SLOW DOWN!"

"I just want to know how you did it!" he said then, before Quinn could answer, a voice from behind them interrupted.

"Yes! I think the world would like to know, how did you do it, Quinn?"

The voice belonged to a tiny woman with a fierce wit and a sharp tongue. Behind her loomed a large camera which focused in on Quinn's face, as it appeared on the giant screens on the arena walls.

"Um, I don't know really," said Quinn, looking at their friends nervously.

Taylor and Joy nodded at Quinn. They watched as Quinn looked around, reaching into their pockets to find comfort in the familiar dice. Then Quinn seemed to relax, their shoulders dropped and they stepped forward, looking her straight in the eye.

“I used a combination of scientific methods plus a thorough assessment of the ground surrounding the golden marker to calculate the momentum and force needed to propel the shot at the correct speed and angle.”

“Beyond that, I guess I was just lucky,” concluded Quinn and they turned away. As the journalist and her camera moved to follow them, Sally, their unofficial official stepped in saying, “Sorry but the Dirtbags will take no more questions at this time, as they must now prepare for Round Two.” She paused and looked around, continuing, “I, however, saw the whole thing.” And with that Quinn, Taylor and Joy left Sally to enjoy her fifteen minutes of fame.

Eleven

The Dirtbags walked over to their rest zone, which was flanked with Dirtbags flags and banners, as well as having Dirtbags merchandise all over the place. Taylor picked up a cup with his face on it and filled it with a green fizzy liquid.

"How weird is this?" he said and took a sip. "Wow, this stuff is amazing!" He went to refill it but Joy stopped him.

"Taylor, it's your turn next, remember, so not too many bubbles, OK?"

Taylor's face dropped a little. "Oh right, yeah, me next."

Just then a low rumble came from underneath the stadium and the Dirtbags turned towards the scoring circle. As they did, huge rods that looked like spears emerged from the centre of each marker, rising towards the sky, transforming the arena, ready for Round Two.

The tallest of them all was the Golden Spear.

The sound from the crowd died down and over on the other side of the stadium the Mavericks came together in a very serious-looking huddle.

"What are they doing?" said Quinn.

"They must be having a team talk," said Taylor. "Let's have a TEAM TALK." So the Dirtbags all stood together looking awkward.

"What do we talk about?" said Joy.

"I dunno," said Taylor, pausing for a moment before he looked into Joy's face with wide eyes.

Joy reached over and gave him a huge hug. "You are going to be awesome." Then Quinn joined in and three of them crushed each other in preparation.

The three friends pulled apart just in time, as Sally came rushing over.

"Righto," she said. "Well done, Quinn, that last move was truly unbelievable, but this round is a bit more of a challenge, so you'd do well to take notes and concentrate." It seemed that Sally had now taken it upon herself to become the Dirtbags' unofficial coach as well as their unofficial official.

"She's right," said Quinn. "We've done the first round, but there are two more to go."

"Exactly," said Sally, pulling the Dirtbags into a huddle.

"OK, so as you know, this round is Rings of Fire, Taylor's speciality."

"It is?" said Taylor and then received a dig in the ribs from Joy. "Right, yes, it is," he said, rubbing his side.

"Yeah, all you have to do is get the tyres over the scoring spears. The challenge is the tyres themselves, but you know that." Sally smiled knowingly, then pointed to a stack of tyres that had appeared at the side of the arena, just next to the slingshot platform. The tyres looked entirely normal as in HUGE and HEAVY.

"I don't know," said Taylor, with a shrug, turning away so Sally couldn't hear, "I'm not known for my upper body strength. He gave a weak smile and stuffed his hands in his pockets. "Miss Balls says I'm useless at pushups. Well, she says I'm useless at everything actually."

Taylor grazed the floor with this shoe. Joy poked him and he smiled. "Just do your best," she said, "that's what my mum says," but before Taylor could respond, a loud whistle rang throughout the stadium.

"WELCOME BACK TO THE ZENTROPIAN GRAND FINAL! IT'S TIME FOR ROUND TWO! WITH ONE ROUND IN THE BAG, WILL THE DIRTBAGS CONTINUE THEIR WINNING STREAK OR CAN THE MAVERICKS STEAL THE SHOW WITH RINGS OF FIRE?"

Taylor twisted his hands over and over, wondering how he was ever going to lift the tyres that were stacked beside him, AND WHAT WAS THE FIRE BIT?

"FIRST UP IS TAYLOR!"

"What?" cried Taylor, then whispered to Joy and Quinn, "I thought the Mavericks would be going first. What do I do?"

The two friends stood silently for a moment then Quinn turned to Taylor.

"So, it's just like Dunkin Doughnuts, OK? Just think about it like that. You just need to get the doughnut –" Quinn pointed to the tyres – "over the spear –" pointing to the giant rods that rose towards the sky. "See?!"

"Except you don't eat these," said Joy. Taylor grimaced.

Everyone seemed to be waiting and Taylor suddenly became very aware that they were waiting for him to do something.

Sally nodded and gestured towards the pile of tyres.

"Go on, Taylor," she said, "you'll smash it!"

Taylor wandered over to the tyres, trying to look purposeful and heroic. When he got there, he placed his hand on the top one and to his huge surprise the tyre gave way beneath his palm. The black surface seemed to shimmer with iridescent colours and move as his fingers tapped out a rhythm as he decided on a plan of action, which currently included running and hiding.

The crowd started to clap, slowly at first and then faster and faster. Taylor felt a whoosh and his head began to spin, thoughts whirring through his mind, thoughts he had a thousand times before.

What if I look stupid? What if I can't do it? What if I fail?

A rumble in the distance snapped Taylor back into the present and he gasped as the clouds above Chromicron seemed to crackle and light up from within. Taylor thought back to Joe's store, the storm and the unexpected journey through the portal. He remembered flying and the fear that lived in the pit of his stomach but had now moved up into his mouth. He looked at his friends and a new feeling emerged as he remembered that all that had happened and, despite all of the doubts and the fears, here they stood, the Dirtbags, underdogs of the championship, friends for life, and he knew that no matter what these two would never judge him because they didn't care what he did, they just loved who he was. He smiled and reached for the first tyre.

Taylor looked around the scoring circle and tried to see how he might get the maximum points. The green spears were the furthest away and you needed to get a lot of height to get the tyre over the top whereas the red were closer and lower. Even so, Taylor just couldn't imagine getting the tyre in the air at all. Just then Sally appeared at his side.

"I know you know this, Taylor, but just thought I'd remind you that the tyres will go a lot higher in these conditions, you know, with the wind and everything." She tapped the side of her nose, like they'd just shared an official secret and Taylor nodded wisely.

At that point the whistle was blown and the official gestured Taylor forward onto a large platform that, when he stepped on to it, rose into the air, making the crowd cheer and Taylor grip the metal sides just a little too hard. The tyre rested against his body and came up to his waist and when the platform came to its resting point, Taylor realised that he was level with the yellow spears, meaning he had the choice of throwing upwards to green or aiming downwards to gain thirty on the red. Equally there was a Yellow spear in his eyeline, just a few feet away and this suddenly seemed like the most obvious choice.

Taylor gripped either side of the tyre and felt it shift in his hands. As he lifted it above his head, the crowd gave a huge cheer and a rush of excitement shot through Taylor's body.

He made a quarter turn so that he was facing the stands, he widened his stance and began to crouch, tyre held aloft.

"What's he doing?" said Quinn to Joy, both of whom were craning their necks to see Taylor on the platform. "Is he OK?"

"I think he's thinking it's like shot put?" said Joy. "You know when you have to spin before you throw?"

"Will that work?" asked Quinn but was just met with a shrug from Joy who was squinting into the sky to see what was happening.

What was happening was that Taylor was about to launch his first shot in Rings of Fire and, in a very unexpected development, he suddenly felt entirely sure of what he was doing. He shifted his weight onto his back leg, brought his shoulders round so his entire body was facing away from the scoring circle. His goal, the yellow spear lay just in front of the platform, perpendicular to both Taylor and the tyre.

"Just throw it straight," said Taylor to himself, he closed his eyes. "It's Dunkin Doughnuts."

He took a deep breath, gripped the type, turned and released it into the sky.

And it flew.

But to Taylor's horror, as the tyre took to the sky, it transformed from its solid form into a glistening and fluid mass, twisting and turning in the breeze and floating high above each of the spears. This shapeshifter continued its journey way beyond the scoring circle and over the heads of the crowds, and Taylor watched, both fascinated and dismayed, as they jumped and called, trying to catch it, as if it was a runaway balloon. Eventually the shot disappeared out of the stadium, only to be enveloped in the dark clouds which continued to growl and shudder from the hills.

Joy and Quinn were stunned.

"Oh my god," said Joy, "how will he ever get it over the spears? I mean, it doesn't move like anything I've ever seen."

But Quinn stood silent, not knowing what to say and how to help his friend, who now looked tiny and very alone on a platform in the sky.

Taylor was thinking exactly the same as Joy, *How do I know how to throw this thing?" How do I score?*

He looked up and saw the giant screens replaying his last shot, the shimmering formation moving this way and that until it glided out of sight. Taylor slumped for a moment and then began to move towards the ground as the platform descended to where his friends were ready to meet him.

At the bottom, Quinn and Joy rushed forward, Taylor went to leave the platform but instead was presented with his second tyre and, just like that, the platform began its climb once more. Taylor felt lost. He needed to speak to his friends. He needed Quinn to tell him what to do. He needed Joy to hold his hand and tell him he'd be OK.

Taylor slumped onto the tyre, which rested on the floor of the rising platform. Now it was just him. Just him, high in the sky, ready to fail.

The platform ended its journey and once again Taylor was level with the spears, looking round to each one and trying to make a decision about what to do. Should he go for the golden spear – like Quinn had gone for the golden marker? But Taylor wasn't smart like Quinn, he didn't see the world in calculations and angles, Taylor's world was colour and creation, joy and freedom. Some of the most beautiful things Taylor had even drawn had started as nothing. A doodle in the corner of a page, a wibbly face that became a rose or a painted wall.

Sometimes he just had to let go of an idea to let another take shape.

So that was it!

He needed to let go. Taylor sat up straight and shook his head, waking himself up to the present moment and what he needed to do.

"Just let go," he said to himself, smiling, and without waiting he picked up the second tyre and dropped it over the side, watching it as it shifted and shone, taking on a new form, second by second.

The crowd was holding its breath as the tyre seemed to plummet towards the ground, passing the green and yellow spears and heading into a non-scoring zone but then suddenly, as if it caught a breeze, the neon mass now rose and spun, moving further out, climbing higher and as it did, the crowd began to clap. Slowly at first but then, as it rose higher and higher, the clap was joined by stamping feet and cheers which grew louder and louder. The giant screens flickered with action and the cameras followed the cloud of light as it began to dip. Now it was amongst the spears, green to its right, yellow to the left. Scattered below were several reds, and the glowing formation seemed to float and tease as it drifted down, veering left and right.

Taylor, Sally, Quinn and Joy were standing, mouths open, hearts racing; Taylor thirty feet in the air, Quinn and Joy firmly rooted to the floor, Sally pacing in the rest area, cup in hand.

A cheer erupted from all four, as Taylor's second shot hovered for a moment over a yellow spear, just to the right of

Taylor's platform, and then, as it made contact, to their astonishment its glittering formation immediately became a solid mass once more, plummeting to the floor beneath and exploding into a cascade of fire as it hit the ground.

The entire stadium rose to their feet and Quinn, Taylor and Joy watched in amazement as the fire subsided to reveal nothing at the base of the spear, not a shred of the magical creation that had left Taylor's hands moments before.

"FIFTY POINTS!"

Taylor had scored and it felt AMAZING! He gripped onto the metal barrier as the platform whizzed him back to earth and he stepped off into the arms of his two best friends.

"Brilliant, Taylor!" said Joy, hugging him tight.

"Well done, buddy," said Quinn, "that was crazy!"

No sooner had Taylor said thanks then his final shot was loaded onto the platform. As he entered, Taylor looked around at the crowd and, in a very un-Taylor move, he ran his hands through his hair and then pointed to the sky, much to their delight.

As he whizzed upwards to take his final shot, Taylor realised that he was grinning from ear to ear with pride.

The platform quickly finished its journey and once again Taylor stood amongst the spears, looking from green to yellow, then red, knowing that the decision was not his to make. As before, Taylor understood that the mysterious mass would make its own journey and that all he needed to do was let go and believe. He picked up his final tyre and marvelled as it began to respond to the warmth of his hands, already beginning its transformation. He stepped to the edge of the platform, closed his eyes and released it into the air.

This time, the tyre seemed to ride the wind, circling the scoring zone, sometimes edging towards the crowds. Children leaned out to try and touch it, only to be pulled back by agitated parents, who continued to wave their flags and track the ever-changing form as it sparkled blue, yellow and gold.

Taylor was hoping for maximum points on this shot. With the yellow he'd earned the Dirtbags fifty points but he was hoping to get the full eighty and give his team the best chance in the tournament. He looked over to see his shot dipping low, out of reach of the green but heading again towards the yellow. The crowd saw this too and started a low cheer.

"Woooooooooooooooooooh…"

Taylor closed his eyes, waiting for the sound to erupt but instead the crowd went silent and he opened his eyes to see the flashing and feathery orb floating down again, skimming the tops of the red markers. At each one Taylor felt his heart stop and his breath shorten; the crowd seemed to beat out the rhythm of its journey with their *oooh*s and *ahhhh*s.

A red would be fine, Taylor thought, a red would still be great but as his final shot came to rest, Taylor realised that it had reached a no scoring zone. No points, no fire just a HUGE AND HEAVY black tyre sitting amongst the spears and ending Taylor's chance to score.

The crowd's disappointment was palpable. They slumped back into the stands and let out a collective sigh. Taylor stood, still high in the sky but instead of feeling like a champion he now felt exposed and vulnerable. He clung onto the metal guard and willed the platform to start its descent but instead it continued to hold him up for the world to see.

Down on the ground, Quinn and Joy felt Taylor's pain and looked upwards to see when he would begin his journey. His head hung low and looked round at the faces in the crowds.

"Taylor, Taylor, TAYLOR!" Joy started to chant.

"Joy?" said Quinn quickly, "What are you doing?"

"He needs this, Quinn, come on", she said, then, "TAYLOR! TAYLOR! TAYLOR!", loudly. She started clapping her hands.

Sally was the next to catch on and she rushed over to join Quinn and Joy, and soon members of the crowd were chanting and clapping Taylor's name too.

"This is still a victory," said Joy, in between chanting. "Taylor has won our team fifty points! Fifty points! And before that we had none," she cried out towards the sky. "Taylor, you've won!"

As if the announcer had heard, suddenly a voice boomed out:

"THE DIRTBAGS FINISH THE ROUND WITH FIFTY POINTS TAKING THEM INTO THE LEAD! IT'S ALL UP TO THE MAVERICKS NOW, CAN THEY CLAW THEIR WAY BACK TO VICTORY? FIND OUT NEXT AS STARZI TAKES TO THE PLATFORM. BUT NOW GIVE IT UP FOR TAYLOR!"

And now the crowd rose to their feet and at last Taylor felt the platform move and the faces of his friends came into view. For a moment Taylor felt all the familiar pangs of his daily life but now he stepped off the platform as a winner, knowing that he'd done his best and trusted himself to try, and that was everything.

No sooner had he stepped off the platform than Sally bounded over, beating Quinn and Joy and taking all three of them off swiftly to the rest area. She pulled them into a huddle and leaned in, voice low.

"OK, nice work Taylor, you've got us some points on the board BUT I've just heard that the Mavericks are bringing something or SOMEONE new to the table for this round. Apparently they've been working on some fancy techniques."

"What kind of technique could possibly work?" said Taylor. "These tyres have a mind of their own!"

"Yes, traditionally, Rings of Fire has always been the unpredictable round due to the lack of control," agreed Sally. "In fact there have been a few petitions started to try and get it removed from the games as many felt it was a bit pointless –" she paused for effect – "sometimes literally."

Sally laughed briefly and looked around at the three blank faces.

"So why have they kept it?" asked Joy

"It's a crowd pleaser," she said and rolled her eyes. "The magical transformation… the fire…"

"Right," said Quinn, "that was REALLY COOL THOUGH!"

"YEAH!"

And the three of them started talking over each other in excited voices, sharing everything they had seen, thought and felt during Taylor's Rings of Fire round. Until…

"AND NOW IT'S TIME TO WELCOME THE MAVERICKS TO STEP UP AND PLAY

RINGS OF FIRE!"

The Dirtbags looked over to the Mavericks as a tiny figure with a determined look on her face approached the platform and was whisked into the air. As it came to rest, over the heads of the spectators, Taylor, Joy and Quinn were able to catch sight of the new player.

"She looks familiar," said Joy,

Taylor nodded, "I agree, there is something about her."

"More importantly," interrupted Quinn, "what is she going to do?"

"And what will that mean for us," said Sally, as if from nowhere.

As before, the giant black tyre sat beside the player and, as round one was announced, Maverick Starzi went to take her first shot. However, unlike Taylor, she did not place her hand on the outside of the tyre but instead hooked her arm through. Contact made, the tyre took on its shimmering form and the tiny player lifted her arm towards the sky. With the dark clouds as a backdrop, the translucent formation glittered and glimmered as everyone waited with bated breath.

"Well, well," said Sally nodding sagely, "I never thought I'd see the day."

"What?" asked the Dirtbags in unison.

"This technique," she said, "it's not new, in fact it's very, very old. Goes back to ancient times."

"And does it work?" said Quinn, feeling impatient as they looked to the sky.

"Oh yes, it's very effective. I never really understood why it was rejected but the new wave of players seemed to want to do their own thing so it kind of went out of fashion."

It would seem that Sally was not the only one who remembered this technique. A growing swell of murmurs became *ooh*s and *ahh*s from the crowd as Starzi began to rotate her arm, causing the fluid mass to follow its movement and regain some of its original structure. This apparently was the key to success, according to Sally, who was now waxing lyrical about the pros and cons of this technique which was called Rod of Steel. However, none of the Dirtbags were listening; they became transfixed by the increasingly hypnotic effect of the spinning light. The crowd were equally in awe as Starzi moved faster and faster, shifting her position on the platform by degrees until she was perpendicular to the scoring circle.

Now she began to bend at the knee, crouching low but maintaining her arm rotation, the spinning slowed a little and then in a well-practised and swift move, she flung the shot off, towards the outer spears, aiming for the highest possible score for the Mavericks.

At this point, Joy and Quinn were expecting the shot to drift and follow the breeze just as it had with Taylor but instead it continued its trajectory straight towards the green spear top.

“Why is doing that?” said Taylor, to no one in particular.

Quinn answered, “I think it’s got something to do with how she created momentum within the object and because her arm was inside the ring the entire time, it remained kind of structured?”

“Bang on, Quinn,” said Sally. “Many believed it was magic when it was first used but really it was just physics.”

“Riiiiiiggggghhhhttt,” said Taylor and Joy, looking at Sally and Quinn like they were talking in French.

But there was no time for chatting as Starzi’s shot continued to make its way directly to the outer circle, looped itself onto the first green spear and immediately fell to earth, bursting into flames triumphantly as it landed.

On the other side of the arena, the Mavericks went absolutely crazy, all except Catcher Day who stood in the centre of the commotion, arms crossed, looking up at Starzi, making small gestures with his hands, ending with a thumbs up. Taylor looked up and saw Starzi nod and answer with a thumbs up as she began to move towards the ground.

Meanwhile the stadium had exploded into celebrations, streamers criss-crossed in the sky and the Mavericks’ theme tune blasted out from the speakers. Whilst her team mates danced and congratulated themselves, Starzi remained focused and, for a moment as she turned to collect her second shot, she caught Joy’s eye and smiled.

“Well, that’s it then,” said Taylor, who suddenly felt like all his efforts were for nothing, “they’ve won. That’s eighty points.”

This was true. With this first shot, Starzi had claimed this round as a victory, beating Taylor's fifty points with her first score. However she had two shots to go and, in true Maverick style, she finished the round having taken out all three green markers, totalling 240 points. The Rod of Steel was now firmly back in fashion and the Mavericks drew even with the Dirtbags as they finished Round Two with one victory each.

The stage was set for the final showdown.

"It's all up to you now," said Sally, as the announcer called Joy's name.

Twelve

"NEXT UP AND FOR OUR FINAL ROUND WE HAVE RINGS OF GLORY! DIRTBAG JOY AND MAVERICK CATCHER DAY GO HEAD TO HEAD IN THIS RACE FOR VICTORY. NEVER IN THE HISTORY OF THE TOURNAMENT HAVE WE WITNESSED SUCH A CLOSE COMPETITION. WITH ONE ROUND EACH, IT ALL ENDS HERE WITH RINGS OF GLORY!"

And with that the band sprang to life and the cheerleaders entered the stadium once more to entertain the crowds as the arena was reset for this final round.

The Dirtbags retreated to their rest area, Joy keeping a close eye on the action to try and determine what was in store but Taylor slumped immediately into one of the beanbags emblazoned with the Dirtbags logo, and Quinn soon joined him.

Taylor looked devastated and, seeing this, Joy left her lookout position and came over to support her friend. Quinn and Taylor were already deep in conversation.

"B-but how could I have known about th-the arm thing?" Taylor stammered. "I've never even played this before but then Sally was saying it was my speciality and now this with Joy and we don't even know why we are here. I mean why is all this happening?"

Taylor was becoming increasingly agitated and, as his mood darkened, the clouds around the hills in the distance began to crackle and groan.

"I never even wanted to be here! I didn't want to fly through a portal and play a stupid game that I DON'T EVEN UNDERSTAND!" , by this time Taylor was shouting, first at his friends but then at the sky, a dark anger filling his soul. "Is this what you wanted, Joe? Is this IT?" He screamed this last sentence to the sky, arms flung open, his voice drowned out by the band and the constant cheers of the cheerleading squad who were flipping and turning with every beat.

Tears filled Taylor's eyes and at first Quinn and Joy felt powerless, unable to help. Quinn felt a pang of guilt for persuading them all to go on this adventure, an adventure that Quinn so badly craved but now wondered, had they done the right thing? Was it possible that instead of an adventure Quinn had taken them somewhere full of failure and disappointment?

Joy stood motionless and watched as the clouds continued to growl and expand, seemingly growing darker and more malevolent as the moments passed. Taylor's sobs filled the air and as the cameras zoomed around the arena, Taylor crouched and turned, hands in pockets, hiding his face, afraid of what the crowd would see.

Joy walked over to where Taylor was now curled into a corner and put her arms around him, sheltering him from view. The dark clouds spat with rain which drifted in the wind and sprinkled over the crowds, causing screams of delight from young children who were growing tired as they waited for action.

"It's OK, Taylor," said Joy, "you're OK. I've got you. I've 100% got you."

"Through his tears came Taylor's voice, cracking and broken, "Why is this happening, Joy? Why did Joe bring us here?"

Before Joy could answer, Taylor continued, now quietly with such sadness that it broke Joy's heart, "I don't need to go to some magical place to play a game and feel like a loser –" he hesitated – "because I already feel like one every single day of my life. In class, in the corridors, in PE, sometimes at home." This last bit he said almost as a whisper because it was hard to admit.

"Me too," came a voice from the other side of the rest zone. Quinn stood up from their own place in the darkness and joined their friends in the corner.

"I feel like this every day, Taylor. Everyday. My dad doesn't really know me and sometimes I feel like he wishes I'd disappear. The only place I really feel OK is with you. With you and Joy, hanging at Old Joe's. I loved it when he was still alive, when the four of us were together." Quinn went quiet.

"The five of us, you mean," said Joy suddenly. "You mean FIVE."

And with that she smiled and, after a moment, this smile crept onto Quinn's face. They nudged Taylor, who looked up, tears streaking his face, "Can't forget Captain America!"

A tiny smile played on Taylor's lips.

"Remember when we dressed him up as the real Captain America to make Joe smile?" said Quinn

"And how much Joe loved the picture on the counter, Taylor, the one you drew for him?"

Taylor went quiet again "I wish he'd really seen it but by the time I'd finished it, he was already gone. I mean he was still there, upstairs, mostly, but he was gone really, he was gone." A single tear slid down Taylor's cheek.

The Dirtbags sat in silence.

"But he loved it, Taylor," said Quinn. "Sometimes I would find him tracing the outline of it with his finger, over and over, smiling and talking to himself. I could never understand what he said but whatever it was it was said with love."

"He loved you, Taylor. He loved us all," said Joy, "and not because we painted him a picture or made his sandwiches. He loved us because of who we were. Who we are. The Dirtbags. His Dirtbags."

"He loved the fact that when we walked into the shop, you would almost always knock something over, Taylor, and Joy couldn't ever stop talking." Quinn smiled

"He loved the fact that we were always together and would bring a trail of Cheeto dust into the shop." Joy looked at Quinn. "He loved us not because we were perfect or successful but because we were losers. Amazing losers!"

"THE GREATEST LOSERS OF ALL TIME!" said Joy and did a little spin.

By this time the Dirtbags were lost in their own world but as Joy spun in the air she became conscious that the cameras had captured every moment and the crowd were waiting to see if the Dirtbags were going to rise to the challenge. Suddenly a tiny voice pierced through the sound of the band, "I love you, Taylor!"

Taylor looked round to see the boy who he had spoken to when they first arrived at the stadium. The boy was waving the picture that Taylor had signed for him and then hugging it to his chest, like it was a prize. Taylor stood and wiped his face, waving at the boy, and Quinn joined him, then Joy came flying in from behind and now the Dirtbags were centre stage, together, showing everyone that friendship, love and truth don't make you perfect but they can make you awesome.

A chant began and soon the whole stadium was cheering and waving, some for the Dirtbags, some for the Mavericks, and sadness and worry turned to hope and excitement as the final round began.

■■

The rules of Rings of Glory were pretty simple. It was a sort of all or nothing game.

The arena now had been transformed and, instead of the spears from the previous round, there were just two hoops set high up on poles, at opposite ends of the scoring zone. Scattered around the 'court' were poles of differing heights. These poles were once the green, yellow and red markers, and had become obstacles that each team had to navigate to gain success. The goal was this: first to score wins and, in this case, wins the entire tournament and ultimate glory, The Zentropian Gold.

Rules for play were as follows:

Only one player from each team could score. For the Dirtbags this was Joy and she was facing the Maverick Captain, Catcher Day.

The scorer could be assisted by their teammates, who could run ahead, provide distractions and even work against the other team's efforts. It could be a dirty game.

Any obstacle within the scoring zone could be used by any team member but you could not make contact with the hoop itself. Doing so would result in no score and a sixty-second timeout, which could cost you the game AND the tournament.

Joy stood, hands on hips, at the outer edge of the court, wondering how she was going to make this work. The hoops were high above her head, towering into the sky, and she was reminded of all those appalling games of netball in PE when she had failed to score and ended up, as usual, being reassigned to ball monitor whilst all the other girls got to run around the court.

Quinn stood behind Joy and considered the task, Taylor beside them. Joy turned to them.

"So, what's our plan, how are we going to do this?" she asked, hoping one of them might have an idea.

Quinn and Taylor both shrugged and the three of them turned to see the Maverick team warming up on the other side. Catcher Day seemed to be pointing to various poles in sequence and then Catcher, Starzi and Troy turned inwards and brought their heads together, deep in conversation, no doubt plotting their route to victory.

Joy grabbed the shoulders of her two friends and pulled them towards her.

"Come on, let's at least look like we know what we are doing."

“But we don’t,” said Quinn and paused.

After a while, Taylor spoke, “But I think that’s OK.” He started to grin. “In fact, I think it's our superpower!”

Joy and Quinn blinked at Taylor, who was hopping from foot to foot with a wide-eyed look of excitement on his face.

“That’s it, remember! We never planned any of this – like we didn’t even plan to meet each other, or find Joe, or fly through a portal, it just happened!”

Quinn caught his drift and continued, “So let’s trust ourselves and just go in and see what happens, yes?”

“Yes! I mean what’s the worst that can happen, we lose? Uh, hello, we are incredibly good at losing!” said Joy, laughing.

“World’s best losers.”

“SUPERHERO LOSERS!”

They fell about laughing until suddenly Sally was tapping them all on the shoulder and hurrying them towards the court, wishing them good luck.

As they approached the playing area, Quinn stopped short and cried out,” Wait!” Joy and Taylor hurried to their side, worried that something was wrong but Quinn was grinning.

“What is it?” said Joy, quietly, aware that the world was watching.

“It’s parkour, Joy,” said Quinn and looked at her, eyebrow raised, “IT’S PARKOUR!”

Quinn started to point across the arena with growing excitement.

"This –" they pointed to one of the smaller red obstacles – "is the first rack in Old Joe's." They gestured to a taller yellow. "And this is the second."

Joy suddenly saw it. "Oh my gosh, so that –" she pointed across the zone – "is the sofa and that is the counter!"

"Yes, Joy, YES!"

"This is it, Joy, you've got this and we've got you, just tell us where you need us to be."

"OK," said Joy as they continued their journey towards the arena, "just be ready, it's still going to be tricky and I'm going to move fast so concentrate and focus."

"LET'S DO THIS."

"WELCOME BACK AND HERE WE GO. IT'S THE FINAL ROUND OF THE GRAND ZENTROPIAN TOURNAMENT AND, IN THE TIGHTEST RACE IN HISTORY, IT ALL COMES DOWN TO THIS.

IT'S ALL OR NOTHING OUT HERE FOR OUR TWO TEAMS SO LET'S GIVE IT UP FOR THE MAVERICKS!"

The crowd went crazy, screams of "Catcher, Starzi, we love you!" flew through the sky.

"AND THE DIRTBAGS!"

At this a huge cloud of orange dust erupted in the stands as Quinn's fans went wild and all around the stadium, flags and banners flapped and fluttered in the wind.

The sky grew dark.

“THE RULES ARE SIMPLE, FIRST TO SCORE WINS THE GAME AND WINS THE TOURNAMENT! MAVERICKS, ARE YOU READY?”

The Maverick camp went wild in response, hollering and cheering, the crowd egging them on.

“DIRTBAGS, ARE YOU READY?”

Not really, thought Joy, but the crowd started chanting and soon Taylor, Joy and Quinn were waving, and spinning to the delight of the people who were willing them to do well. The loudest voice belonged to Sally, who had now ditched her official uniform and was dressed head to toe in Dirtbags merch.

The teams took up their positions on the court, Catcher Day seemed poised and ready, eyes on the prize, ready to strike. His teammates were placed at even intervals and Joy watched as they continued to gesture and signal to one another.

This could be over very quickly, thought Joy, wondering what the hell she was going to do but before she had time to panic or plan, the whistle sounded and they were off.

First move from the Mavericks was swift. Catcher leapt forward and Troy immediately knelt down allowing Catcher to springboard off him and deflect off the nearest post to make a shot.

The Dirtbags watched in horror as the Mavericks’ ball glided towards the gold hoop but then a huge wave of relief washed over them all as it hit the backboard and ricocheted back out into the scoring zone.

This gave Joy an idea and a second later she launched herself into the space, hurtling towards Taylor, hoping like mad that he understood what he needed to do. Taylor saw Joy and immediately copied Troy, kneeling down to allow Joy to step onto his back but as she did he pushed upwards, giving her a mighty push into the air and Joy spun and twisted above their heads, landing atop one of the tallest poles in the stadium. The golden hoop sat a few feet away, glistening against the sky.

Meanwhile beneath her feet, the Mavericks were gearing up for their second shot and suddenly Quinn tapped Taylor on the shoulder.

"Come on," they said with urgency, "we've got her up there, now it's up to her but we can still stop them, remember!"

Taylor smiled and the two friends high fived before running towards the Mavericks in an effort to distract them from their well-executed plans. Taylor circled Troy, kicking up dust and shouting, like he was trying to frighten a bear away. Quinn targeted Starzi, who was now heading towards Catcher Day, arms outstretched, Quinn attempted to divert her but she was focused and, as she reached him, she and Catcher linked arms and she spun him round like a shot put and he careered off towards the pole that lay opposite Joy.

So now, Catcher Day and Joy were standing on either side of the golden hoop, both ready to shoot in this impossible game of chicken. The same thought was running through both their heads. '*If I jump and shoot, there's nowhere to go but down*', and the fall was too great, too risky, even for this, the ultimate prize.

The only way was to stand and shoot and hope that your ball got there first.

GO!

Catcher and Joy flung their balls forward, heading for the hoop, but Catcher's was faster, and, for a moment, the entire stadium held their breath, waiting for the shot to drop and the final bell to sound.

But instead, the Maverick's ball overshot the hoop, knocking Joy's out of the way then hitting the side of the hoop before plummeting the ground. Catcher hesitated; disappointment covered his face but Joy didn't want to lose a minute. In an instant she turned and spun away from the pole on which she stood, deftly moving back down, jumping from pole to pole, green, yellow, red until she landed next to Quinn and Taylor.

Without hesitation she pulled them close and gave them their orders, she knew exactly what to do. EXACTLY. And she took no time in giving instructions to her friends. Then she ran towards the gold pole as Joy sped to collect her shot.

With equal urgency, Catcher had now regrouped and dispatched Starzi and Troy to new points in the arena. Both him and Joy leapt onto the lowest red obstacle before them, Catcher then hopping to yellow, but Joy remained at red for a moment waiting for her signal from her teammates.

Now Starzi threw the shot to Catcher who was poised ready to shoot but her first attempt failed and she scrambled to find it as it hit the ground, creating a dust cloud all around it. Meanwhile Troy had decided to tackle Quinn, moving in front of them time and time again, stopping Quinn from taking up their position, delaying the signal and Joy's next move.

Starzi had now found the shot and took a moment to focus before getting ready to throw to Catcher. She knew she needed to get this right.

Joy waited and waited, watching as Quinn's efforts to get into position were thwarted by Troy.

And now Catcher had the ball.

"Help them!" cried Joy. "Taylor, help Quinn NOW!"

And Taylor did, he ran as fast as he could and barged into Troy, like he'd seen but never done before. Troy stumbled backwards and Taylor pulled Quinn into position, hands clamped together, knees bent low at the foot of the golden hoop.

Joy took her moment and leapt into the air, praying with everything she had that this would work.

It had to work.

Her feet made contact with her friends' hands, firmly intertwined, and, as they did, Quinn and Taylor lifted and flung Joy upwards with every ounce of strength they had.

Catcher moved to make the shot, the ball left his hand and arced its way towards the hoop as Joy spiralled through the sky.

Joy was flying again, she was light and air and without knowing how she twisted and spun upwards, ball in hand until the hoop came into sight.

Catcher's ball circled the hoop, teetering on the edge for a moment before slowly dropping through as, with one final flip, Joy rotated above the golden hoop and slammed the ball through the ring before landing, feet together, on the platform behind.

BOOM!

The Maverick camp went crazy, with the Dirtbag fans chiming in just a nano second later.

Who had won? Whose shot was first?

The crowd fell silent as a group of officials, including the chief tournament official, came together in a very serious-looking huddle.

The Mavericks were quick to respond, whipping up their fans into a frenzy, clapping their hands faster and faster, but Sally, who had now joined Taylor and Quinn in the circle, insisted that Joy's shot had been faster therefore she should win.

"I saw it, clear as day," she said, "it shot through and was clear of the hoop BEFORE Catcher's so we should win."

And with this Sally lifted her arm and started her own chant, willing the Dirtbags to victory.

Joy bounced down and was greeted by her friends.

"What's going on?" she said urgently, looking round to see officials scurrying by, some carrying large books titled THE RULES.

"I don't know," answered Quinn, "but, Joy, whatever happens, I'm so proud of you, that flip was just awesome, never seen anything like it. We were like 'Woooaaahhh', and the crowd were like 'Oooooohhh', weren't they, Taylor?" Quinn looked round to see their friend staring off into the distance. "Taylor?"

Joy and Quinn came over to join Taylor and watched as the dark clouds surrounding the Chromicron hills began to bulge and bend with life. The friends gasped as what looked like a face seemed to appear in the crackle of lightning that shot through the sky. Almost immediately the giant screens whirred to life and Sally came running into view.

“They are using VR!” she said, puffing as she reached them. “Apparently the shots were so close that there is no way to make a decision so they need to watch it in slow motion to decide. Ultimately the shot that leaves the basket first WINS!”

The Dirtbags turned their faces to look at the screens, and the entire stadium waited and watched.

The screen on the right was going to show the Maverick’s shot, and Catcher Day stood underneath it, flanked by Starzi and Troy, their faces lifted to the screens.

Taylor, Joy and Quinn moved towards the screen on the left and as they gripped each other’s hands, the final moments of this tournament began, in slow motion.

Joy was just a blur on the screen as the replay showed her leaping and flying through the air. It came to the shots from both teams and there it was, as clear as day, Joy’s shot leaving the basket nano-seconds before Catcher’s.

A cry erupted from the crowd but then there was a flurry of movement in the officials’ camp and suddenly the image on the Dirtbags’ screen was being replayed again, back to Joy’s final flip over the hoop before she scored. This time the footage was enhanced and the hoop came into clear view. The picture slowed down into super-slow motion and gasps of horror ricocheted around the arena as Joy’s hand came into shot, upside down but as she passed above the hoop, her little finger caught it, touching it just for a moment. Joy let out a tiny, “No,” and the crowd went silent.

THE PICTURE WAS FROZEN.

Everyone stopped, some with heads hung low, others’ eyes sparkling, waiting for the announcement to come.

The tournament’s top official climbed onto the platform and addressed the crowd.

“Thank you for your patience. The tournament officials have reviewed the footage, and it is the unanimous decision that Dirtbag player Joy made contact with the golden hoop, and this is a violation of rule 1.4 in the tournament handbook.”

There was a murmur through the crowd and Joy looked across the stadium to where Catcher Day was shaking hands with Troy and his other teammates. But Starzi looked over at Joy and smiled, mouthing, “Sorry.” Joy smiled back and realised that she was OK. She didn’t feel crushed or upset, she just felt exhilarated and proud of herself, of both of her friends. Her smile deepened and she turned back to Taylor and Quinn, giving them a huge hug. As she did, the voice boomed from the speakers, making them all jump.

“THE WINNERS OF THE FINAL OF THE GRAND ZENTROPIAN TOURNAMENT ARE… THE MAVERICKS!”

Thirteen

There was absolutely no time for the Dirtbags to feel bad or talk about disappointment or failure because as soon as the announcement came the entire stadium erupted into joyful cheers, music and dancing!

People streamed from everywhere to come and congratulate Taylor, Joy and Quinn, high-fiving each one of them, asking Quinn how they had hit the golden marker, quizzing Taylor about what the weird tyres felt like and telling Joy how amazing her gymnastics had been in the final round.

The Dirtbags felt amazing, like superheroes, like they each had a superpower and they'd just discovered it. They felt like they'd won gold.

As the celebrations continued an army of tournament officials, including Sally, worked quickly and efficiently to construct the platform for the winners' ceremony. Minutes later the klaxon went off and the band started playing the tournament theme music. The Dirtbags turned round to see the most glorious, golden structure, sitting right in the centre of the arena, stairs of every colour leading up to it as it glistened amongst the bright lights of the arena.

"Woah," said Quinn, "that is epic!"

The platform was enormous and had two beautiful, adorned levels. The winners' level was decked out in the Mavericks' trademark colours and, as the music continued, the team congregated at the bottom of their steps, holding a rich velvet flag embossed with the Mavericks' logo. Catcher Day stood at the front of the line, flanked by his teammates Starzi and Troy as well as their coaches, all ready to climb the steps to victory.

As they stood and watched, Sally suddenly appeared next to them, dusting down her Dirtbags uniform and holding their own beautiful flag, bright with the Dirtbags' colours and logo. She handed it to Taylor.

"Thanks, Sally," he said, "but I don't think I should hold it…" He faltered, just for a moment. "I think it should be Quinn or Joy. They really shone today."

"Why don't we all do it?" said Joy.

"Yeah," said Quinn, "let's do it as a team."

"The best team," said Taylor, eyes shining, grinning from ear to ear.

So as the tournament band played and the crowd sang and cheered and clapped, both teams began to climb, ready to take their places in Zentropian history.

Whilst the Mavericks were led by Catcher all the way, the Dirtbags did it their own way, with Quinn taking the lead, holding the flag out front, proudly stepping forward. Then Taylor came up, taking the flag from Quinn and leading the way as they passed the halfway mark. Then finally Joy, handed the flag by Taylor, climbed the last few steps and triumphantly placed the flag in its huge golden holder, and all three watched and waved to the crowd as their flag gently flapped in the wind.

Once both teams were in place, the band took on a new energy and the cheerleaders bounced into the arena, flanking the tournament officials as they walked towards the middle staircase, ready to join the teams and complete this epic tournament.

The atmosphere in the stadium was electric, Quinn felt everything at once – overwhelmed, excited, proud. They felt a pang of sadness for a moment, knowing that this was something that their dad would have loved, wondering if they would ever share this kind of excitement together again, but then Joy squeezed their hand and Taylor rested his head on their shoulder and the three friends took a collective breath, taking it in, loving it all.

The officials reached the pinnacle of the platform and immediately all sound and movement in the stadium stopped and an expectant silence fell.

The top official stepped forward and addressed the crowd.

"THANK YOU, EVERYONE, FOR MAKING THIS EVENT SO SPECIAL. IT'S BEEN A PLEASURE TO WELCOME YOU ALL TO THE BEAUTIFUL ZENTROPIAN STADIUM! THIS YEAR HAS SEEN ONE OF THE MOST HOTLY CONTESTED COMPETITIONS, A JOURNEY OF EMOTIONS AND ACTION. I THANK BOTH TEAMS FOR MAKING THIS A NAIL-BITING ROLLERCOASTER TO THE END. THANK YOU!"

The crowd went wild, clapping and cheering, shouting the names of their favourite players.

The speakers crackled and an army of officials moved into position in front of the Dirtbags

"SO, WITHOUT FURTHER ADO, WE PRESENT THE MEDALS TO OUR TOURNAMENT RUNNERS-UP, THE DIRTBAGS!"

Taylor, Joy and Quinn stepped onto the small platforms in front of them and bent their heads low to receive their medals.

Sally, as one of the officials, couldn't help but give a small squeak, as she slipped it over Quinn's head and, as they stood back up, they gave her a cheeky eyebrow which made her laugh out loud.

The crowd showed their appreciation for these valiant competitors and Taylor, Joy and Quinn returned the love by waving, jumping, smiling and cheering.

They looked down at their medals and each one of them swelled with pride, amazed at what they had been able to achieve. They stopped and turned to each other, engulfed each other in the biggest hug ever and then watched as the officials approached the Mavericks, who stepped up onto their platforms and waved to the crowds around.

“NOW IT GIVES ME ENORMOUS PLEASURE TO PRESENT THE GREATEST OF ACHIEVEMENTS, THE ZENTROPIAN GOLD, TO THE REIGNING CHAMPIONS. NOW FOUR TIME WINNERS, PLEASE GIVE IT UP FOR THE MAVERICKS!”

And now the entire stadium rose to their feet, the applause sounded like thunder. Feet banged all around them and the Dirtbags stood, spellbound in the centre of it all, grinning as the Mavericks received their medals, joining the crowd in stamping and clapping, so alive in that moment of glory.

“So, what happens now?” said Taylor, shouting above the sound that surrounded them, which seemed to be getting louder and more intense with every second.

“What do you mean?” asked Joy.

“I mean, what now… the portal, the shop… school?” His face fell for a minute.

“Yeah… I don’t… know, actually,” said Quinn, looking up at the sky, “I…”

But at that moment they were drowned out by the most enormous bang, an explosion that seemed to come from directly above the stadium.

Everyone looked up, expecting to see the bright colours of fireworks, sparkling and raining over the crowds, marking the end of this spectacular event, but instead they watched as a growling and ever-increasing cloud of darkness came into view, above the arena, like a tide of fear and horror, crackling and creaking as it blocked out every shred of light, and threw the stadium into total blackout.

There were cries from the crowd and then lightning seemed to explode in the centre of the darkness. The entire stadium let out a huge collective gasp as a face seemed to appear, for the briefest of moments while light shot through the clouds which now seemed alive. Alive with monstrous energy, feeding from the fear that surrounded it.

In the darkness, the Dirtbags could hear children crying and, although an announcement came over the speakers, it went unheard, muffled by the thick dark air that invaded every corner of the arena.

Suddenly, the Dirtbags each felt a hand grab them and they could barely make out the figure of Sally as they groped for each other amidst the darkness, beckoning them to move and run.

Joy realised that all around her, she could hear the sound of people fleeing, footsteps banging and crashing as they made their way down the staircases, first tentatively and then quicker, fuelled by fear, fear of the unknown force that seemed to be gathering pace above them and all around.

The noise increased and was now deafening, a terrifying mix of screams from beneath the platforms and deep groaning from the sky, punctuated by streams of electricity that emanated from within.

Quinn, Taylor and Joy shouted at each other, trying to work out what to do. They huddled together as they raced down the staircase and watched with horror as they realised that the ground beneath them was a mass of movement, people running, sheltering from this unknown terror.

As Quinn and Joy reached the ground, they looked back to realise that Taylor was still midway down, facing the sky, hands stuffed into his pockets.

“TAYLOR!” Joy screamed at the top of her voice. “TAYLOR!”

Taylor turned, his face streaked with tears. Quinn and Joy rushed back to his side as he collapsed against them, crying, “It’s all my fault, it’s all my fault,” his voice disappearing into the wind that howled around them.

“WHAT?” shouted Quinn, their face inches away from Taylor’s. “TAYLOR! WHAT DID YOU SAY?”

“I SAID IT WAS ME! IT’S ALL ME! I MADE THIS, I MADE THIS HAPPEN, I CREATED THIS WORLD, THE DARKNESS, CHROMICRON, IT’S ALL BECAUSE OF ME!”

He stood and shouted into the darkness. Joy pulled him towards the ground and the three sat, faces together, arms around each other, in their own bubble of safety, whilst hell raged above their heads.

“We all felt it, Taylor. We all have darkness inside of us. You didn’t create it,” said Joy into Taylor’s ear. “When Joe died, we all lost ourselves for a bit.”

“Yeah,” continued Quinn, “one day he was there and everything was good and then he just wasn’t any more.” Quinn looked at their friends. “And I was angry. So angry with him for just leaving us. For never even telling us how ill he was. We could have helped. I would have. I would have looked after him every day.”

"But he never even gave us a chance," said Taylor, his face full of emotion. "I've never felt like that before, all that sadness and anger, and I guess I just… I just…"

"Had to put it somewhere," said Joy, squeezing his hand. "You had to put it somewhere, Taylor."

"But it was just a drawing, a corner of this world that I started when I met you all, at Old Joe's and it was never meant to become… to do this…"

He stopped talking and the three of them looked up to the sky which loomed above them, black and menacing, heavy rain now falling, the stadium in darkness.

Suddenly out of the corner of her eye Joy caught a glimpse of the young girl who had made her smile when she first entered the stadium. The girl saw Joy too and for a moment stopped, the look on her face full of uncertainty and fear. She raised her hand to Joy and then was gone, ushered towards safety by her parent.

Joy sat for a moment and looked at her two friends, both now lost in a world of memory and sadness. Above her head, the sky matched every emotion that raged through their bodies, each tear that fell.

Joy closed her eyes and took a breath, and in one moment she knew what she needed to do. She stood, her hands leaving Taylor's and Quinn's, and began to climb the staircase which had once – led her to the greatest triumph of her life, but now took her ever closer to something different, darker.

As they realised what was happening, Quinn and Taylor called after her, "JOY, JOY! WHAT ARE YOU DOING?"

But Joy was now running up the stairs, taking two at a time, sure of her pathway, heart racing.

As she continued her ascent, more people who were now cowering in the stands watched and started to call out. The Mavericks stood together on the perimeter, Catcher Day stepping forward, joined by Troy and Starzi as Joy reached the top of the platform and silence descended. The only sound was the low growl which came from the very centre of the dark mass, now inches from Joy's face.

Joy was terrified. For a moment every fibre of her body was filled with doubt. Every moment that she had been laughed at and bullied, told that she couldn't win, that she was a joke; every failure played in her mind like a movie. But then those images were replaced by flying and twisting, golden moments of joy and love, crowds cheering, waving and dancing and feeling loved, feeling so very loved, and as these images filled her head, Joy began to dance.

At first, it was small, her shoulders moving to a rhythm that was building inside her, rushing into her muscles, spreading slowly through her body and, as it spread, Joy began to smile.

Her eyes were closed, her body swaying, feet moving from side to side, hips alive, the music that only she could hear now loud, present, unmistakeable.

The crowds stood, stunned. Some still huddled together, others rising from their seats to watch as this brave young girl danced against the darkness.

"Look!" cried a voice, suddenly piercing the silence, and the entire stadium looked on as the clouds that were once almost touching Joy's face began to retreat, slowly recoiling from the light that was starting to emanate from Joy, who was now lost, lost to her rhythm, her body moving in a beautiful and unique way.

Taylor and Quinn were spellbound, transfixed by what was unfolding in front of them, a heady mix of fear and pride swelling through their bodies.

The clouds above their heads continued to retreat, as if repelled by the positivity that Joy was creating.

"She's making joy!" said Quinn suddenly. "That's what she's doing, Taylor"

"What?"

"Chromicron was built on darkness, on sadness, but Joy, Joy is fighting it, look! She's fighting it with love and light!"

Without knowing it, Joy had now risen into the air and begun to shine. Arms outstretched, she spun through the air, twisting and turning, dancing, moving.

Joy continued to dance, getting faster and faster, spinning through the air. She was glowing, making traces with her hands as she moved. The entire stadium gasped as she rose higher, the clouds above her now feet away, retreating but still lingering like an omnipotent force, growling and groaning as Joy flipped through 360 degrees like she'd been thrown by unseen hands. She rose higher and higher and then suddenly began her descent, now completely surrounded by an iridescent golden glow, the earth coming up to meet her.

The clouds continued to press into the sky above the scared and confused crowds, and the Mavericks, Taylor and Quinn looked over to Joy and then went wide-eyed when, as if she held the power of the sun itself, Joy landed with a huge BOOM and rooted herself deep into the ground.

The clouds began crying and screaming, rushing now towards Joy and the earth beneath, trying to swallow the land in darkness.

As they hurtled towards her, Joy lifted her hands, which shone like gold, and roared towards the sky.

Light streamed from Joy and began to penetrate the clouds above. Screams and whines started to surround the stadium and seemed to be coming from the clouds which now writhed as if in pain.

“My god,” said Taylor, “it’s alive!”

Quinn took his hand and they looked on as Joy continued to hold the clouds at bay with her strength, and then she began to shake, her feet leaving the ground once more.

Quinn and Taylor rushed forward, concerned for their friend.

"Joy! Joy!" they shouted but she couldn't hear them, she was lost to the light, spinning in the air.

"Taylor!" Quinn said desperately. "What do we do?" They shook their friend, trying to get some help.

But Taylor was staring up deep into the heart of the dark clouds.

Quinn moved closer to Joy.

It was like she was being held by a force that they couldn't see, her hands shaking hard, her light fading, her body becoming limp. Quinn gasped as they realised that, gripped tight beneath her fingers was the trophy that had been in Joe's shoebox, the one that Joy had held as she flew through the portal.

"TAYLOR!" Quinn shouted and pointed it out to Taylor. "What do we do? I feel like it's here for a reason."

Taylor was focused on the clouds, lost for a minute, but then he suddenly turned to Quinn.

"There's a gap!" he shouted, coming forward so Quinn could hear him. "There's a gap. When I drew it, I drew a gap, at the heart of it, like a moment of hope. Like Joe always teaches us."

"What does that mean, Taylor? We need to act now – look! Look at Joy!"

They both turned to look at their friend who seemed tiny as she hung in the air, the wind whipping around her.

"We need to get the trophy to the heart. Send it straight into the middle of the clouds." Taylor looked around. "We can use that." He pointed to the slingshot that Quinn had used in the first round of the tournament. Then it had sat at the centre of the arena but now it was turned away from the scoring circle, pushed back into a corner during rounds two and three.

Quinn and Taylor ran to the giant slingshot and began to pull and push it, trying their hardest to drag it towards the circle so that Quinn could make the shot.

But the slingshot was heavy, made of wood, steel and layered with gold. Quinn and Taylor moved it only a few inches before collapsing on the floor.

"We'll never make it. It's too heavy." Quinn gasped, tears filling their eyes as they watched their friend grow smaller and smaller against the darkening sky.

"We have to try, Quinn. We have to," said Taylor, pushing his shoulder against the unforgiving structure, willing it to budge.

Now, the crowds turned their attention to the two friends and soon everyone in the stadium was looking on as Quinn and Taylor struggled alone in their desperate attempt to save their friend. Finally the news reached the Mavericks and one by one they came out from where they were cowering, full of fear, away from the darkness.

In a split second Starzi made the decision and began to run across the circle and towards the Dirtbags. She was followed at once by Troy, and then finally by Catcher Day, all belting across the arena to help Taylor and Quinn.

As they reached the slingshot, they all pushed together, rivalry set aside, and slowly the slingshot began to turn. But they were running out of time and they knew it. The clouds were starting to descend once more and Joy's light was almost gone.

"It has to be now!" yelled Quinn. "Taylor! Or it's too late!"

"Everyone, push after three," shouted Taylor, his voice barely audible above the dark and ominous groans coming from the sky. "One… two…"

"Three!" As they all pushed forward, Sally and a team of tournament officials joined the cause and, in one final movement, the slingshot swung into position.

Quick as a flash, Quinn stepped up onto the platform, knowing that this was it. Just like the golden marker, the time was now and the window of opportunity was closing.

Taylor stepped up and joined them and squinted into the sky, pointing frantically into the centre.

"Follow my finger, Quinn, it's there, it's right there."

Quinn followed the line of Taylor's finger and saw a tiny flash of blue, a beacon of light amongst a sea of darkness.

They placed the trophy into the shot, stepped back, hands in, legs rooted. Quinn arched their back and moved the shot backwards, using every ounce of strength they had. The clouds shifted and vaulted above the stadium. Quinn took a breath and took the shot.

The trophy sprang from the slingshot with a powerful force, as though driven now by the collective goodness that emanated from every single person that lived and breathed in that moment. The entire stadium held its breath. Quinn and Taylor rushed towards their friend as the trophy was propelled into the clouds. Starzi, Sally and the rest of the team all held each other as the trophy seemed to disappear into the sky, consumed by the darkness and then…

All at once the sky exploded. Light seemed to pour from everywhere, blinding them all for one single moment and then slowly, like sunrise after a stormy night, the crowds watched in disbelief as one by one the clouds disappeared and the sky became a mass of blue, like crystal, gleaming with the promise of a brand-new day.

Joy fell to the floor then opened her eyes as the world came into focus. She felt weary and light, her heart was racing. She looked down at her hands which had traces of light dancing around her fingertips and then, in a rush of movement, she was surrounded by her two greatest friends, enveloped in their arms, their voices rushing through her brain like music.

Before she could speak, the crowd from every corner started to chant.

"Dirtbags, DIRTBAGS! DIRTBAGS!"

Joy looked around, at the beauty of the day, the memory of darkness and anger flashing briefly infront of her eyes before being driven away by the sights and sounds coming from all around her.

And then suddenly Starzi appeared in front of her, taking her hand.

"Joy, I want you to have this," she said, smiling, "I've never known anyone as brave as you are. You are courageous and unique and you dance to your own rhythm. Your soul is beautiful, Joy. It's beautiful."

And with that she placed the Zentropian gold around Joy's neck and the entire stadium erupted with noise. Clamouring for their instruments, the band began to play and suddenly from every part of the arena, the sky exploded with streamers of glorious colour.

It rained down on them all, Joy, Taylor and Quinn, three friends, holding on to each other at the end of this incredible journey.

And as the streamers fell, a small shred of golden paper drifted down and landed on Quinn's nose. They took it off and held it out for Joy and Taylor to see.

"*The Amazing Adventures of Glitterman*," said Quinn and, for a moment, their eyes filled with tears, Reminding them of the grumpy but kind old man who had given them the greatest adventure of their lives.

"Thanks Joe" Quinn said and reached for the dice, "What now?"

The three friends looked around and took in this glorious moment once more, all three knowing more about themselves than ever before, what they can be, what they can do but more than anything, knowing that being who they are, and only that, is enough.

The Dirtbags stood together and raised their hands, bringing together the trophy, the dice and the locket once more.

"Shall we?" said Quinn. And they were gone.

Fourteen

Epilogue

“Do you think they’ll notice?” said Taylor.

“Notice what?” asked Quinn.

“You know, that we’re different?”

“Are we?” said Joy. ”I don’t think we’re different. I mean, your hair looks as bad as usual and Quinn’s face is still mostly orange.”

Taylor rolled his eyes but smiled and Joy poked him as they continued to walk to school.

“Do you feel different?” said Quinn, licking their fingers which were covered in Cheeto dust. “I mean, what happened was pretty crazy.”

Before Joy or Taylor could answer they heard the familiar tones of Mrs Doobetter at the school gates, accompanied by the standard small child,

“Taylor,” she called as he ducked behind his friends. The headteacher stepped in front of the group and Taylor poked his head out from behind Joy.

“Ah, Taylor,” she said, enthusiastically, “I’d like you to take our new student on a tour of the school this morning, I’ve cleared it with your teachers, so no need to worry!”

Taylor stopped, looked up at Mrs Doobetter and took a deep breath.

"Actually, Mrs Doobetter, if it's OK, I'd like to go to my classes this morning. I have double art today and it is my favourite lesson. Plus I'm beginning a brand new project today with Mr Fineline and I think it would make it tricky if I missed the first session. Joy and Quinn could take Peter around the school. I think they'd do a really good job."

Silence.

Mrs Doobetter looked completely flummoxed and, for a moment, the Dirtbags wondered if she was going to laugh or cry, her face reflecting a range of emotions from minute to minute. Then, to their relief her face broke into a smile as she turned back to Taylor.

"Righto," she said. "That seems like a great idea. Thank you, Taylor, and enjoy your art lesson!"

As Taylor walked through the school gates, Mrs Doobetter brought the small boy over. "Quinn, is it? And Joy? Would you mind showing Peter around? I'd be very grateful. It's his first day."

And so Joy and Quinn got to miss their first lesson, they showed Peter all the boring but necessary bits ie: lockers, classrooms etc… but also introduced him to the hideouts, the shortcuts, AND took him to see Taylor in art where he spent a lot of time saying "WOAH".

So, a good morning.

As they settled down to lunch in the canteen, the Dirtbags looked around and realised that maybe school was OK, not TOO bad, not hell (at least) and Quinn opened their Cheetos with a grin and a big cloud of orange dust.

Suddenly in the far corner of the canteen a large group of students gathered around a table, surrounding it and picking on an unseen target in front of them. As the noise continued to rise, others in the area joined them and soon what looked like a mob was jeering and shouting, locked shoulder to shoulder as a small figure tried to fight their way through them and out to find safety.

The Dirtbags looked over, remembered the times when it was their turn and for a moment their eyes met, ready to gather their stuff and leave.

"It's Peter," said Joy, catching sight of the small boy they had helped that morning. "Look!"

Peter was crouched, on top of the table at this point, kids all around him, holding his bag and emptying his lunchbox.

Joy had seen enough.

"STOP!" she screamed at the top of her voice and started crossing the canteen at speed. Taylor and Quinn stood and followed her, unsure of what was coming.

As Joy approached the corner of the canteen she realised that there was no way she would be able to get to Peter through the mob that was now three to four rows deep of kids, all calling and cackling at Peter's discomfort.

In one clean move Joy leapt up onto a table that was in front of her, plates and cutlery clattering to the ground noisily, and made her way across the room, table by table, students leaping out of the way, the mob slowly becoming aware of the ninja movement that was coming their way.

But there was still no way through and Peter was now off the table and cowering against the wall, tears streaming down his face, his blazer smeared with food from his lunchbox, kids everywhere laughing and pointing.

Joy was desperate to reach him, to protect him. Remembering old wounds, she filled them with the love and light she felt now and launched herself forward, flying through the air, landing cleanly on windowsill above Peter's head and then flipping 360 degrees before landing squarely in front of the baying hoard of blazers, all of whom stopped immediately, stunned into silence.

For a moment Taylor and Quinn held their breath, looking on from behind the mob and desperately hoping that Joy was not going to become the new target, but then there was a flurry of activity as a number of teachers and lunchtime supervisors entered the canteen and the crowd automatically dispersed, desperate not to get caught and put in detention.

Joy climbed down to Peter, quickly joined by Taylor and Quinn who retrieved his books and bag, cleaning up his blazer and handing him over to Mr Kindfull, the head of pastoral care, who gently comforted the boy and took him somewhere quiet to catch his breath. The Dirtbags knew that at some point they would be called to his office to 'have a chat' about what had happened but for now they just felt happy that they had done the right thing and stepped in when needed.

"Maybe we are different," said Quinn as they went back to their table, the noise and chatter still buzzing around them.

Suddenly Joy felt a tap on her shoulder and she turned to see Amber, Simon, George and Freya from the cheerleading squad.

"Joy, that was amazing!" said Amber, stepping forward and smiling at Joy. "Just amazing. I never knew, well I mean, we never knew you could do that. I wish you'd done that at tryouts."

Joy nodded, unsure of what to say.

Amber looked at her teammates and then back to Joy.

"Well, look, the thing is, we really need a new flyer. The last one, well, it didn't work out and I know the tryouts didn't go so well for you Joy, but we wondered, if you like to join, you know, the squad and be our flyer?" Amber looked at Joy expectantly, Georgie and Freya grinning and nodding behind her. Simon Bateman raised his head and looked at Joy.

Taylor and Quinn stepped forward and stood with their friend, feeling good in this new and uncharted territory.

Joy thought for a moment and looked at everyone around her, waiting for her to speak. She closed her eyes and listened, knowing that the answer was within her. She breathed and opened her eyes.

"Thanks but I'm kind of busy at the moment," she said. "We – " Joy held onto Taylor and Quinn's hands – "have got some stuff going on and it's kinda important, so I just won't have the time." She smiled widely at Amber and the team. "Thanks for asking though."

And with that the bell rang. Everyone rushed to get to their next lesson and the Dirtbags grabbed their bags.

As they headed off in different directions, Quinn, Taylor and Joy took a moment to come together.

“What you got now?” said Quinn.

“PE,” said Taylor grimly.

“Oh, come on, Taylor, it might not be so bad,” said Joy as she turned to Quinn. “See you at Old Joe’s?”

Quinn produced the twenty-sided dice from their pocket and saw Zentropian Gold glint from inside Joy’s blazer.

“Sure, I’ll see you there.” And they raised an eyebrow.

Above their heads the sky crackled and the Dirtbags laughed out loud.

“See you then, Old Joe,” they all said, then raced off down the corridors, ready for a new adventure.

Printed in Great Britain
by Amazon

32978449R00079